Vermont
SAINTS & SINNERS

Lee Dana Goodman

Vermont
SAINTS & SINNERS

An impressive assortment of geniuses, nincompoops, curmudgeons, scurvy knaves, and characters

Lee Dana Goodman

NEW ENGLAND PRESS
Shelburne, Vermont

ISBN: 0-933050-32-1
Library of Congress Catalog Card Number: 85-72569
Printed in the United States of America
First Edition

The New England Press
P. O. Box 575
Shelburne, Vermont 05482

Cover by Andrea Gray

Photo credits: p.7, Courtesy of the Rhode Island Historical Society; p.31 (top), Collection of the Vermont Historical Society; p.31, (bottom), Courtesy of Dartmouth College; p.56, Courtesy of National Life of Vermont; p.97, Courtesy of U. S. Department of Interior, National Park Service; p.102, Courtesy of the Vermont Historical Society; pp.144-145, Courtesy Amy Bentley Hunt, the Jericho Historical Society, and Mary G. Lighthall.

To Myra Gray Goodman
my mentor and resident critic.

Acknowledgments

Like motherhood, historical writing is self-taught. However, its conception is possible only through the interaction of such fertile purveyors of knowledge as witnesses, other historians, researchers, and librarians.

This, then, is to voice my gratitude to all those who so productively aided my pursuit of history with their cooperation, patience, and expertise. A roster of these collaborators follows:

. . . Vivian Bryan, formerly Division Director of the Vermont Department of Libraries at Montpelier. Her diligence in tracking down texts and documents should have been measured by the distance covered in those multi-corridored stacks. Indeed, if she had been paid by the mile, she would have been able to retire years earlier. It was she who put me on the trail of Rufus Streeter's murderer (to oblige a Missouri descendant who had hoped to have his ancestor exonerated of the crime for which he was hanged).

. . . The tradition of unstinting service and expertise is maintained by Mrs. Bryan's successors, Greg McCandless and Paul Donovan. By processing microfilms with their photostatic wizardry, they often trapped obscure and elusive data vital to my research.

. . . The Vermont Historical Society's library staff members Laura P. (Peggy) Abbott and Mary Pat Brigham. Their familiarity with Vermont genealogy and history is an invaluable complement to the library's extensive resources.

. . . Those unnamed but not unsung guardians of criminal records and vital statistics secreted in the microfilm library of Vermont's—not always—Public Records Department. They coped with my visits with commendable civility, yet with a wary eye.

. . . West Windsor's peripatetic historian, Mary Fenn, author of *Parish And Town: The History of West Windsor,* whose memory and files were an abundant resource.

. . . Windsor's librarian, Gail Furnas, an adept expediter of books throughout the state, and a purveyor of obscure minutiae. Her encyclopedic knowledge was a memory bank as readily available to me as her phone number.

. . . The Springfield Library's Ellen Graf who tipped me off to the whereabouts of a privately owned book not otherwise available.

. . . Those diligent members of numerous community historical societies whose files were open for my scrutiny; and to others like Windsor's Beatrice Dana. Her extensive chronicles and clippings of family and town were a treasure-trove of historical data.

. . . The denizens of Dartmouth's Baker Library were often conspiratorially cooperative in allowing me access to its archives.

Preface

The theft of firewood is far more prevalent in Vermont than in New York City, whereas the crime rate in Vermont's subway system is non-existent because there are no subways. This proves one major point and one minor contention: Crime is often environmentally determined, and Vermont's environment has bred a special variety of saints and sinners. Its specialness has also produced an impressive assortment of geniuses, nice people, nincompoops, curmudgeons, scurvy knaves, and others collectively identified as characters. They animate Vermont's history.

Some of them make their entrances and exits in this volume. The trials of saints and the trespasses of sinners, plus the more ordinary triumphs and tribulations of ordinary folk, are the gist of this book. *Vermont Saints and Sinners,* therefore, is a portrait sampling of diverse characters presented in their respective historical frames of reference.

First a word about these historical frames and the relevance of history to life. Tension is, of course, the essence of life. It dictates man's destiny. Without tension there would be no effort, and therefore no success or failure (which so often is the humus for ultimate achievement). Serenity would reign. The saga of serenity would merely be a chronicle of inertia, and thus of stagnation. Existence would only be a prolonged yawn. There could be none of the dynamic forces that are the catalysts of history. History, then, is a rearview image of man's progress for good or ill. It exposes both man's noble and ignoble nature. What makes history three dimensional is our ability to experience it vicariously, yet safely, from the distance of time. Surely this is more pleasant than being confronted with our own contemporary truths. That is the concern of sociologists and psychologists, the media and the clergy.

We historians, too, have our duty: namely to sharpen the focus of the past while preserving or restoring its "true" colors within that framework of time and circumstance. Ideally we should be dispassionate and assiduously objective. Realistically we are not. Because like all fallible people, historians cannot be wholly free of bias, any more than a mathematician can measure infinity. Therefore the reader is urged to read between the lines with the vision plus the insights of his or her own sense, and sensibilities, and values. In that spirit, I hope that *Vermont Saints and Sinners* will prove to be a rewarding encounter.

Contents

Vermont
SAINTS & SINNERS

The Cannon Cavalcade

History, which is to say fate, is often determined by the incongruities of circumstance. This contention is illustrated by the following chain of events that significantly affected the outcome of the American Revolution:

On May 10, 1775, that patriot, rascal, and land speculator Ethan Allen, along with Benedict Arnold (later a traitor) and three hundred of their Green Mountain Boys, captured Fort Ticonderoga.

On March 17, 1776, the British evacuated Boston. It was the surrender of Fort Ticonderoga that ultimately liberated Boston from the Redcoats' occupation. If it had not been for the city's deliverance, Vermont and the thirteen original colonies might still be under British rule.

With the capture of the fort, its cannons, mortars, and howitzers, plus ample stores of ammunition (along with the contents of its well-stocked wine cellar), fell into the hands of the stalwart Vermonters. The importance of that prized arsenal can only be appreciated by realizing that the patriots had no navy sufficient to blockade Boston harbor and thus prevent its access to British troop and supply ships. Therefore only by using heavy artillery with a range that made the harbor too risky for the delivery of British reinforcements and war material could the Americans make the Redcoats' presence untenable. No such artillery was readily available, as the regional foundries were in British-held territory.

So desperate was General Washington for such armament that he agreed to an aide's suggestion that it should be brought from Fort Ticonderoga some three hundred miles away. On November 16, 1775, Washington authorized the expenditure of $1,000 for wages, equipment, and supplies (including the hire of horses and oxen) for an expedition under the command of Henry Knox. At that point Knox held no recognized or officially authorized commission. Soon afterward, however, the twenty-five-year-old patriot was appointed a colonel while en route.

By character, intelligence, background, and stamina, Colonel Knox was well qualified for his assignment. He was tall, well-muscled, and personable. Two fingers were missing from his left hand as the result of a shooting accident when younger. A self-made man, he had worked since he was nine as an apprentice in a Boston bookstore. When he was twelve, his father died at sea, and young Knox labored to help support the family. He had taught himself to speak, read, and write French. As a young man he was an acquaintance of such patriots as Samuel and John Adams, Paul Revere, and Joseph Warren.

Colonel Knox's diary is the primary source for an account of his cannon cavalcade. The expedition began with his arrival at Fort Ticonderoga on December 5, 1775. That evening he wrote to General Washington: "The passage across the lake was so precarious that I am afraid it will be ten days at least before I can get them [the armament] on this side of the lake.... The conveyance from here will depend entirely on the sledding. . . . Without good sledding the roads are so gullied it will be impossible to move a sled." That was a mere prelude to the ordeal ahead.

The munitions consisted of 43 cannons, 14 mortars, and 2 howitzers. These 59 units had a total weight of 119,000 pounds (or 59 tons), which did not include the large supply of ammunition. It was all to be transported over both open and frozen lakes, "across frozen rivers, steep mountains," through woods, fields, mud, snow, and over roads that "were little more than rough paths" on wooden sleds and wagons.

Oxen hauled the heavy artillery pieces from the fort to the north landing of Lake George. Despite Colonel Knox's haste, it did indeed take ten days to get his precious cargo to Fort George, for both an overland and water route were necessary. Haste was imperative because of the pressing need for the armament and the threat of bad weather. A sudden freeze could have trapped the expedition at Ticonderoga until spring.

On reaching Lake George, the cargo was removed and stowed on various craft—on scows, a pettiangre (a double-ended boat with a double-mast rigging ideal for maneuvering in limited space), and on a "battoe" (an otherwise unspecified boat). Under the weight of its cargo, a scow ran aground on December 13. The mishap cost the expedition valuable time, but the cargo was saved. As the wind was often against them, they had to rely on the oarsmen's muscle power. It took two days to cross the lake from north to south. On December 15 all the guns had arrived safely at the south end of Lake George. There the boatmen were paid off.

The day before Colonel Knox's arrival at the landing, his younger brother, William, had written that in transporting those weapons in his charge, the boat "got as far as she could get for the ice, for it is frozen a mile which they will have to cut through." Ice was one problem. The lack of snow was another. Without it the sleds were more a hindrance than a help. "The roads [were] so bad," it was reported, "that travelers had to pause every mile or so to rest." The horses tired after trudging only two miles. Then their advance further south from the fort was suddenly plagued by heavy snow with enormous drifts and subzero temperatures.

At Lancing's Ferry, near Albany, the ice on the Hudson River broke beneath the weight of an "18-pounder." But having anticipated such an accident, the cannon had been secured by a long rope which, when retrieved and attached to the traces of two horses, was hauled out. Its recovery took two days of hard work by so many Albany volunteers that the "born-again" cannon was christened The Albany.

With the Lake George crossing on December 17 now well behind them, Colonel Knox "thought the worst of the journey was over." More troubles were just to begin. In addition to the perversity of the weather, Knox had a delicate and difficult problem with George Palmer, a greedy Stillwater contractor who was the expedition's chief supplier. As early as December 12, Colonel Knox had ordered "40 good strong sleds that will each be able to carry a long cannon clear from dragging in the ground and which will weigh 5400 pounds each & likewise that you would procure oxen or horses . . . to drag them." They had not arrived. Instead of the agreed price, Palmer said that he would only make delivery for "an impossibly high fee" to be paid in advance. In a December 17 letter to General Schuyler, his superior officer, Colonel Knox reported that the "500 fathoms of 3-inch rope to fasten the cannons on the sleds" that he also ordered had not been delivered. General Schuyler instructed Colonel Knox to cancel all orders from Palmer "forthwith." The general rightly suspected that the man was a blatant war-profiteer. Palmer refused to permit cancellation of his contract. He claimed that those who were to have provided the labor, materials, and equipment would be so insulted that they would abandon all further aid and loyalty to the patriots' cause. It later was revealed that Palmer was pocketing the difference between the pay the workers willingly took and the amount that Palmer had stipulated in his contract. Palmer "made thinly disguised threats against the convoy," which were potentially troublesome because of Tory feelings in that area.

Soon afterward, however, Colonel Knox hired 124 pair of horses and 62 wagons, plus "42 exceedingly strong sleds" and 80 yoke of oxen "to drag them as far as Springfield (Mass.)." But the sleds were hardly sturdy enough to draw the cannons. Yet on they plodded "over unbroken trails, treacherous ice-covered rivers, mountainous terrain, and muddy, rutted roads."

Those drovers from upper New York state who had struggled to transport the artillery toward Boston refused to go any further than Springfield. Perhaps it was because as "Yorkers" they feared Vermont's Green Mountain Boys, even though men from western Connecticut and Massachusetts also were in their ranks.

Colonel Knox finally reached General Washington's Cambridge headquarters with his "noble train of artillery" intact and right on schedule on January 24, 1776. The journey of some three hundred miles had taken 48 days, an average of 6¼ miles per day.

Some of the cannons were soon positioned at Dorchester

Heights "where the long-range pieces could command most of the harbor and docking area of Boston, thus blocking the main channel." Their presence effectively imposed a blockade of British shipping and, after persistent bombardments, forced the evacuation of all British forces from Boston on March 17, 1776. In the army's triumphant entry into the liberated city, General Washington was accompanied by Colonel Henry Knox.

On the occasion of the nation's bicentennial celebration, the cannon cavalcade was re-enacted. That 1976 expedition, called The Knox Trek, set out on December 10, 1976, with "a token number of eleven artillery pieces in all," hauled on six sledges and in two wagons. The bicentennial caravan retraced the original trek from Fort Ticonderoga to Cambridge as accurately as weather, terrain, and subsequent land and local alterations permitted.

The route went from Fort Ticonderoga down Lake George to Fort George, thence to Glens Falls, Saratoga, and on to Half Moon, from there across the Hudson River to Albany where the Hudson was again crossed en route to Kinderook, from there to Claverack into Massachusetts at Alfred. Then it was on to Otis, Westfield, Springfield, Wilbraham, Brookfield, Worcester, Framingham, and into Cambridge on January 27, 1977.

Stretches of country were broken by asphalt and concrete ribbons bordered by shopping malls, gas and fast-food stations, and by such welcome impediments as flag-waving children, free coffee, doughnuts, pizza, and numerous welcoming committees. Despite these obstacles of exaltation, the Knox Trek reached Cambridge, forty-eight days later, on January 27, in a torrential downpour.

Surely Ethan Allen and his fellow Vermonters must have relished the irony of the British defeat at Boston by their own guns which he and his Green Mountain Boys had seized in their capture of Fort Ticonderoga. There was the additional irony that Vermont's crucial contribution to America's independence occurred sixteen years before Vermont joined the new republic in 1791 as the fourteenth state.

Soldier of Misfortune

Not intentionally was Barton, Vermont, named after Rhode Island's William Barton. No one disputed that he deserved to be honored as a hero for an extraordinary feat. After all, he had captured a British general without his superior officers' knowledge of or consent for that bizarre escapade.

Yet Vermonters, indifferent to his brilliant military deeds, thought that he well deserved his fourteen years imprisonment for debt, or, more accurately, for refusing to pay a paltry fine for some fraudulent business deals. Only the generosity of General Lafayette ended the matter.

With its founding in 1798, the town of Barton got its name by a deception allegedly perpetrated by the brash William Barton himself. The facts of the deception are a fitting prelude to the saga of that soldier of misfortune whose mastery of deception had made him both famous and infamous.

Just before the end of the Revolutionary War some patriotic Yankees, who had fought in Rhode Island and Massachusetts, banded together to get a large tract of land to colonize. Along with patriot William Barton were adventurer Ira Allen (Ethan's brother), John Paul Jones, and Daniel Owen. They presented their plan to the government of Vermont, which then was an independent republic. Their petition stated that the settlement, in Orange

General William Barton (1748-1831), artist unknown.

County, would be named Providence after Rhode Island's capital. In 1781 their petition was approved.

However, it was not until some years later that the new town learned why it had been named Barton instead of Providence. The switch was explained by Abner Allyn, a descendant of the man whom Barton had twice cheated. Allyn reported, according to historian Alton Hall Blackington, that "one of the original petitioners had whipped out his hunting knife, scratched out the word Providence and written in his own name" on the document of incorporation. Despite Abner Allyn's likely bias, his explanation had been widely accepted. Even though it was not a felonious deception, it certainly was worthy of the guile that had forged William Barton's destiny—both for good and evil.

On the stormy night of July 4, 1777, William Barton achieved his moment of glory. He was twenty-nine. Before his enlistment he had developed a flourishing hat shop, had acquired a wife, Rhoda, a child, and a decent house. Galvanized by the *Providence Gazette's* report on the battle of Bunker Hill, he hurriedly left his shop, hearth, and pregnant wife to enlist in General Ward's army, headquartered in Cambridge, Massachusetts. He was soon manning the ramparts at Dorchester Heights. There patriot Barton first saw George Washington. He so admired the general that he named his new son after him.

Barton's resourcefulness, bravery, and ebullient leadership won him Gen. Israel Putnam's recognition in time for the general to give him a commission and appoint him commander of a fort at Tiverton, Rhode Island. It had been hastily built to impede the British from advancing further along the coast.

Barton was outraged by the Redcoats' devastation of such fine towns as Portsmouth, Bristol, and Newport. The British turned Newport's beautiful churches into barracks and stables. The British commanding officer there, Gen. Richard Prescott, had ordered his Hessian troops to cut down for firewood the lovely oaks, elms, and maples that lined the streets. Included were the wooden sidewalks and grave markers.

Wanting more elegant quarters than Newport's Bannister House, General Prescott requisitioned Quaker John Overing's imposing farmstead down the coast a way. Barton had heard of some British deserters and had them brought to him. Their hate for General Prescott served Barton well. The turncoats gave him minute details about the Overing manse and its environs. The information was to prove crucial in his plan to capture the general. None of Barton's fellow officers were informed of the plot. However, he had sought and received the support of enough men so that from among the enthusiastic volunteers for a mission yet to be revealed to them, he was able to choose forty whose knowledge of seamanship was as important as their ability to keep their mouths shut.

Five whaleboats were "borrowed" and provisioned. Each was to be manned by eight soldiers. Barton would be in the first. A violent storm raged as they fought the waves that thrashed Mount Hope Bay. Twenty-six hours later, drenched and exhausted, they reached Hog Island. In the darkness, broken only by the Redcoats' distant campfires, the men rested. Then Barton revealed for the first time the true purpose of the expedition.

Their landfall now made about a mile from the Overing property, Barton deployed some of his raiders to conceal, guard, and ready the boats for a fast escape. He led the others, Indian file, along a footpath that snaked up from the shore to a high knoll where as expected they found the general's farmhouse headquarters guarded by a sentry. Before the Redcoat could fire a warning shot, he was gagged and tied. After posting his raiders around the house to prevent the general's escape, Barton dashed upstairs. As he knew which chamber was the general's, he broke the locked door and seized his prey. General Prescott, naked and drunk, was struggling to don his breeches. He was dragged from the house, and to an accompaniment of alarm bells hustled across a stubbled field; then stowed in the bow of a whaleboat as bullets flew harmlessly overhead.

Barton was compassionate. Once General Prescott was confined to the barracks, he was treated to a hot bath and breakfast. Then, clothed and sober, he was escorted under guard to Providence en route to General Washington's New York headquarters.

Barton's heroic exploit earned him a promotion, the Rhode Island Assembly's vote of thanks, plus the gift of a jeweled sword with inscription presented by a grateful Congress. His military career ended—involuntarily yet heroically—soon afterward. In the spring of 1779 he fought his last battle. While leading his troops against a British attack on Warren, Rhode Island, his hometown, he was badly wounded.

During his long convalescence, Barton was paid a visit by the admiral of the French fleet, Count Rochambeau. Another visitor was the Marquis de Lafayette. The two became close friends. Despite his new status as a noncombatant, William Barton was appointed a general in Rhode Island's militia and a colonel in Washington's Continental Army. Although he had accepted an appointment as a customs officer and was elected to the state's legislature, his civilian life became a progression of disorder, rascality, and disgrace. Whereas he had been hailed as a hero in Rhode Island, Col. William Barton (ret.) was jailed as a scroundrel in Vermont.

Barton had settled comfortably in Warren. Too comfortably. A yearning for adventure, incited by talk of the Green Mountains' beauty and of opportunities to be hewed from its forests and fields, lured him away from Rhoda and the children to northern Vermont's wilderness. He was forty-seven.

Although John Paul Jones and Ira Allen were among his fellow pioneers who had belabored their way into "the promised land" by spanning turbulent streams with flimsy bridges and making corduroy roads of felled trees, they had other schemes elsewhere. Barton, however, settled in a cabin without windows, a floor, or a chimney. He had cleared fourteen acres, and planted three or four with wheat that yielded forty bushels. That was in 1795. The next year he had a flourishing sawmill. In 1798 the settlement was recorded as the town of Barton, his self-proclaimed acknowledgment that he was the town's founder.

Although he had a hand in the town's layout, Barton took no part in its governance, nor did he vote at the first town meeting. Nor did he fetch his wife and children from Rhode Island, as did most of his fellow settlers. His major interests seem to have been the growth of his lumbermill plus the purchase and sale of land.

It was this latter enterprise that ultimately led to his imprisonment. In 1797 he had sold some acreage to Brookfield's Solomon

Wadhams. But the records showed that that land was owned by someone other than Barton. Wadhams sued. He received a $225 judgment against Barton whose tactics of prolonged legal maneuvering kept him out of jail but damaged his reputation. Over the years others were similarily defrauded. The town's first representative, Jonathan Allyn, also was embroiled with Barton in suits over land titles. During this long litigation, other citizens, like William Griswold, also brought suit. Most were awarded judgments. Again Barton was sued by Mr. Allyn "for $3000 and costs." Three court-appointed referees (including William Palmer of Danville, a judge, congressman, and later governor), determined that Mr. Allyn was entitled to "damages of $50.13 and costs of $51.10." Yet Barton refused to pay, even though he could afford to. So the once-honored patriot was jailed. The length of his term was to be determined by how soon he would pay the paltry sum. In 1811 when he started his long residency in the county jail at Danville, he was sixty-three years old. There he stayed for fourteen years until liberated reluctantly by Lafayette's generosity.

Barton's imprisonment was unique. Instead of confinement in a cell, he was restricted to the prison grounds, which were a chain-enclosed area that extended a mile out of town on each of the five roads leading from Danville. The leniency may have been to encourage Barton's escape, for the obligatory imprisonment of such an old and once-esteemed miscreant was an embarrassment to the authorities. Barton chose not to escape; perhaps because the area within his confinement was said to have provided plenty of hunting and fishing. Those fourteen years of imprisonment were "open season" for new and continued litigation. He lost most of the suits. Barton also lost his frequent petitions to Vermont's legislature for his release, for he stubbornly sought exoneration, not a pardon.

It is questionable whether Barton appreciated Lafayette's generosity. His pride had sustained his ego for all those years; years which could have been spent pursuing the fantasies of his megalomania had he deigned to buy freedom with fines that he could easily have paid. To have obtained his release through an old friend's charity was humiliating, especially so when his freedom still denied him the vindication he so persistently had sought as the only honorable route to freedom. Yet to have refused Lafayette's kindness would have insulted his famous friend.

William Barton's civilian years raised more questions than the records can answer. Why, at the peak of his fame, did Barton exile himself to a remote wilderness for thirty years, separated from Rhoda and their children? Why did he not seek and why was he not awarded honors or office in the community that he had founded? Why were Vermonters and prominent Americans generally so indifferent to such an authentic hero that an old man's fourteen-year imprisonment did not raise a public outcry?

His return to his estranged wife and family in Rhode Island was indeed more of a defeat than a deliverance. He was seventy-seven, still proud, still arrogant, still bitter. It is doubtful that in his six remaining years William Barton's presence could have given Rhoda the happiness, peace, and support that his thirty-year absence had denied her. At least the ten years that she lived after his death in 1831, when she was eighty, were made secure by a modest government pension.

It is ironic that Col. William Barton, through deception, gave a town his name to perpetuate the memory of his heroism. Yet because of that town's name, the story of his infamy and reclusive life endures.

Via Stagecoach

Stagecoach. The word conjures a romantic image of pleasant, leisurely travel as pictured in Currier and Ives lithographs of a bucolic world, a world teaming with quaint people too busily engaged in wholesome pursuits of country life to step out of the picture and alert the viewer that "it ain't like it seems."

Stagecoach travel was no pleasure. Take it from Washington Irving. He wrote: "There is a certain relief in change, even though it be from bad to worse; as I have found traveling in a stagecoach, that it is often a comfort to shift one's position and be bruised in a new place."

Such travel was indeed leisurely. Weather permitting, thirty or forty miles could be covered in one day's journey. A passenger could leave Middlebury at 4:00 A.M. on Thursday; be at the Hanover Inn in time for supper, and two days later, Saturday, arrive in Boston. It was a six-hour ride from Rutland's Center Street stable to Woodstock. The stagecoach left at 2:30 P.M., and the one-way fare cost two dollars.

Say "Pico" or "Killington" today and skiing comes to mind. In stagecoach days that long, steep rise or descent was agony rather than ecstasy to horses, coachmen, and passengers. One driver, asked "Does the stage ever fail to get through in winter?" replied, "Only twice last year. Once the gray horse that kicks awfully stood there [in a deep snow-filled trough], with the stage stuck fast and never moved while we dug him clear."

Inevitably there were accidents. The Boston-Montreal stage-coach, reported a Rutland newspaper, "overturned at the narrow Point of Rocks . . . and killed two English gentlemen on their way to Montreal." The steepness and abrupt pitches impelled the coach drivers to heed the advice, "Put your trust in God till the breeching [harness strap] breaks."

When a coach sank to its hubs in mud or ruts, the passengers were asked to get out. The menfolk were expected to free it. Sometimes they refused, for they traveled in their best clothes. On one occasion when the horses failed to pull the coach loose, the driver asked his passengers to alight. Defiantly they stayed put. Thereupon the driver sat by the roadside, filled and lit his pipe, and let his passengers' impatience and concern build up a head of steam which exploded in protests, some of which were launched with profanity. The driver declared, "Since them hosses can't pull thet kerrige out o' thet mud-hole an' ye won't help, I'm a-goin' to wait till the mud-hole dries up." Whereupon the passengers literally put their shoulders to the wheel and thereby disproved a law of physics. For in *that* instance, inertia did indeed generate momentum.

Coach drivers, like today's jockeys and basketball giants, were a special breed. More colorful than their coaches, they were robust, resourceful, tireless, popular, and profane. A sharp vocabulary was as much a part of their function as the crack of their whips to motivate two, four, or six horses.

Vermont's isolation, which had kept it predominantly rural, was predestined by its topography. A major mountain range extends along its entire length like a spine. Parallel minor ranges have intervening valleys, crisscrossed by numerous swift rivers that flow north and south, east and west. Such features, plus extensive forest cover, made travel in Vermont difficult and often hazardous. After spring floods, large sections of the roads were washed out, or merely "were all right enough for a foot-path." Descents were as arduous and often more perilous than the upgrade. In addition to the perversities of nature, man's use and abuse of the roads added to the hazards. Wagons loaded with prime growth logs cut up the roads.

Because Vermont was such a topographical obstacle course, public transportation via stagecoach arrived later than elsewhere in New England. It began about 1796 when the New York City-Burlington route was opened. The trip, made three times per week each way, took three days. The schedules were synchronized with local stagecoach lines so that passengers could go from Bennington as far north as Canada. Way-stops were Manchester, Rutland, Middlebury, Vergennes, Burlington, St. Albans, and Swanton. A rival company, also going from Manhattan to Canada three times a week, went via western New England to Burlington where connections with local lines provided through transit via St. Albans to Quebec's border.

Vermont's first stage "pike," finished in 1779, was intended for military use in case of hostilities with Canada. Instead of facilitating troop movements, "Hazen's Military Road," seventeen years later, became a link in the Boston-to-Montreal coach route.

In 1807 a Burlington-based coach line was founded. Named *The Northern Sentinel,* its stages went from Burlington to Boston. The hard journey began on Wednesday mornings shortly after the stage from St. Albans arrived at 4:00 A.M. The coach pulled into Montpelier at 6:00 P.M.; departed from there at 4:00 A.M. on Thursday; arrived in Royalton at 2:00 P.M.; departed for Lebanon, New Hampshire, an hour later, and arrived there at 7:00 P.M. On Friday morning, again at 4:00 A.M., the stagecoach left Lebanon for Boston, and arrived on Saturday at 4:00 P.M. Time from start to finish: eighty-four hours.

That same year there was tri-weekly stagecoach service between Hanover, New Hampshire, and Boston via Bellows Falls, and return. In 1814, Bellows Falls was also a way-stop for a four-horse Boston-to-Burlington coach. By 1825 seven scheduled stage routes operated between Vermont and Boston. Competition made for better equipment, including sturdier horses, maintenance, schedules, and more favorable rates.

Vermont was webbed by cross-state "turnpikes," that were intersected by regional lines with scheduled trips between such towns as Brattleboro and Bennington, Montpelier-Burlington, St.

Johnsbury-Montpelier, and Newport-Richford. Their schedules connected with those of the major lines. Some of these routes were covered by the popular Concord coaches. They were the Cadillacs of the stagecoach era. Drawn by two or four handsome horses, this stylish coach, made by the Abbot and Downing Company of Concord, New Hampshire, was the ultimate luxury in stagecoach travel.

Because of the coaches' limited capacity, the lines' government contracts to carry and deliver mail were a necessary subsidy. According to historian Julia Kellogg, although frequency of mail delivery was improved, "the whole postal business was run on a basis as informal as a barber shop—no bureaucracy—no hurry. Mail arrived when it arrived." To keep their profitable mail franchise, the operators of a Royalton company paid passengers to ride their stagecoach from South Royalton to Royalton's Fox Stand. Except for the mail, small packages, and the passengers' luggage, stagecoaches carried no freight. Bulk merchandise was transported by packhorses and wagons or sleighs.

To improve statewide public transportation at no cost to the state, Vermont's General Assembly granted charters for private turnpikes intended for stagecoach use. Thus their construction and maintenance, which had to meet state-imposed standards, were solely the responsibility of the individual charter holders. These private turnpikes were supported by the tolls and fees levied on the users. However, the charges were state regulated to maintain uniformity, discourage excessive fees, and encourage use. In 1799, about ninety-one such turnpike charters had been granted. The last charter-holder operated as late as 1917 with one tollgate on the Manchester-Peru road. Peru was the last of the stagecoaches' postroad towns.

Toll collection became increasingly unpopular when the turnpike-chartered companies let their routes succumb to poor maintenance. Finally the towns assumed responsibility for the roads. To provide for their upkeep, a labor draft was imposed. All able-bodied men from sixteen to sixty ("ministers excepted") were required to give four days' labor per year. One driver claimed "the men of Mendon used to work out their taxes on it but now they paid them $2 a day for work on the road and got more done."

Despite the effort, the roads were generally poor. There were three types: gravel, plank, and corduroy, a road made of logs laid crosswise. Boulders, stumps, and washouts made the roads a rough and dangerous obstacle course. Horses were lamed by corduroy roads that "shook the wagons to pieces."

For long trips, horse relays were provided. Woodstock's stagecoach stable kept four horses, while ten were stabled in Rutland. For heavy loads, four horses were harnessed. Usually two were used, but sometimes three. "In this case the lead horse, called Old Tom, was used coming up the mountain, and [coming to Rutland] was turned loose at the top of the mountain, and went the rest of the way direct to the stable by himself, ahead of the stage," according to historian Charles R. Cummings. Without its driver, no combustion-engine vehicle, with many times the horsepower, could equal that feat!

After leaving Rutland, coaches changed horses "about one-half mile from the top of the mountain [Killington] for a fresh pair for the trip to Bridgewater. There they were replaced by two more for the haul to Woodstock. That next morning the same pair would leave Woodstock for Bridgewater, returning in the afternoon with the eastbound stage." Five minute stops were made at post offices in Sherburne, West Bridgewater, Bridgewater Corners, Bridgewater, West Woodstock, and Woodstock. The return trip departed from Woodstock at 6:00 A.M., Bridgewater at 7:30 A.M. to arrive in Rutland at 1:00 P.M.

Coaching stops abounded. Many were inns, commonly called taverns, not more than twenty miles apart. All had barns or stables to quarter the horses and provide fresh teams on a scheduled relay basis. Stagecoach drivers announced their arrivals and departures with trumpet flourishes. They were as welcome and festive as train whistles. Typical of the coaching stops is Calais' Kent Tavern with its taproom and upstairs ballroom. (It is now a museum owned and operated by the Vermont Historical Society.) In addition to lodging, the taverns provided ample food and grog.

Stagecoach travel flourished from the early 1800's to the 1880's, when the expansion of railroad service almost brought the stages to a halt. The stagecoach operators countered by buying

horses with greater stamina and speed. They also provided financing for the betterment of the turnpikes, and they successfully
lobbied for a bigger share of the taxpayers' money for post road
improvement and expansion. However, nothing could impede the
progress of progress, for the competition was shortly to include
the horseless carriage.

One stagecoach driver reported, "Forty-three [automobiles]
passed the stage between Sherburne and Rutland, on the way
over; and one went ahead of 'em throwin' paper like mad. [We]
passed three of 'em afterward laid up along the road by Mendon,
makin' repairs. Had a hoss on the stage that day that used to be
afraid of 'em, but kind of got over it, but when the last of 'em was
goin' by I guess she thought she had delirium tremens—took the
stage right onto the sidewalk on Woodstock Avenue."

It was a fitting end to the era of stagecoaching that passed on
to history's palette of memory, as pictured in artists' romantic
fantasies.

Old Seth Chase

v.

The Poor House

A View of Early New England Welfare

Said old Seth Chase, "I'll starve or freeze to death there [in the woods] before I'll go to that accursed poorhouse!" Except that he was a destitute Vermonter, little is known of Seth Chase. Yet his dread of the poorhouse is amply justified by the evidence.

Almshouses, or poorhouses, which existed in Vermont towns from 1797, were authorized by a law stating that "the inhabitants of any town may build, purchase or hire a house of correction, or work-house, in which to confine and set there to work, vagrants, common beggars, lewd, idle and disorderly persons" and grant permission "to fetter, shackle or whip, not exceeding twenty stripes, any person confined therein who does not perform the labor assigned him or her, or is refractory or disobedient to the lawful commands." Note that no legal distinction was made between the treatment of the poor and the criminals, a fact which may partly have accounted for Seth Chase's loathing.

Because many towns could not afford both a poorhouse and jail, the poor were frequently quartered in the jail. Not until the Act of 1837 did the legislature differentiate between criminals and the poor in the considerations of custodial care. In addition to miscreants, Seth Chase's fellow poorhouse inmates also might have been insane, feebleminded, epileptic, deaf mutes, paralytic, crippled, maimed or deformed, old and infirm, bedridden or blind, according to an early census report.

Perhaps old Seth Chase's problems stemmed from having been a debtor. Before November 3, 1838, when imprisonment for debt was abolished, many poor were jailed as debtors. Thus being denied welfare assistance, they were punished rather than helped. Not even distinguished citizens were exempt from such treatment, (as the case of Gen. William Barton showed in the chapter titled "Soldier of Misfortune").

As early as 1779, the Vermont legislature had passed an act—still in effect—that each town was responsible for "supporting and maintaining" its own poor. To ease the welfare burden on the towns, however, many of which were poor, the legislature passed a blanket settlement law.

"Settlement" was the legal determinant of which town was responsible for its needy citizens. It also specified what qualifications a person needed for relief, such as length of residency in the community. Until 1789 one year was required. However by the Act of 1787, no person "shall gain a settlement in any town in this state . . . unless such person was born therein, or had owned, or shall own, estate [property] in such town, of the value of two hundred pounds, clear of all demands against him or her, or of the yearly value of ten pounds." This was to eliminate vagrants, the influx of immigrants, and welfare cadgers. The poor must have been quite a problem because this act further "empowered a justice of the peace to order the removal of a pauper or dependent to the place of his last legal settlement." It also empowered the constable to deliver the person to the place of settlement.

Seth Chase had little choice but to stay put if he sought relief, for "if any removed person returned to the town from which he was removed, he was to be punished by being whipped, not exceeding ten stripes on the naked back." He not only had to take the Pauper's Oath, which is still obligatory, but no town would give assistance until an investigation determined that there were no relatives with assets "who could be forced to support the indigent person." Assessable relatives included grandparents and grandchildren.

Furthermore, if Seth Chase or the brotherhood of the poor had no responsible relatives, "the court may order or dispose the pauper to any proper work or service under the direction of the selectmen . . . if it were thought that the person's poverty was caused by 'idleness, mismanagement, or bad husbandry,' then the selectmen were to appoint an overseer to manage almost completely the lives of the pauper and his family."

Because Seth Chase was old, we assume that he was infirm. Had he been poor in his youth, he may have been bound out. "Binding out," or indentured service, was a system used by overseers of the poor to place destitute minors out on a contract held between parent (or guardian) and an adult willing to take them on an apprenticeship basis. Such a child was bound out to the master until his twenty-first birthday, or eighteenth, if a girl. Binding out relieved the community of responsibility. It was justified on the basis of a then current theory that "idleness is a sin of the poor, therefore these children of the poor must be put to work as a matter of training and thereby learn habits of thrift and industry." Under this system, child abuse was widespread.

Had Seth Chase also been poor in his prime, he might have been auctioned off to a fellow townsman. For a common way of coping with the poor was to auction off their services. The pauper would go to the lowest bidder for his maintenance. Such was the fate of Joel Titus of Fair Haven. Surely he must have seen some irony in his town's name. In October of 1815, "By a vote of the town, Joel Titus was put up as a town pauper, to the lowest bidder, to find him board and lodging and was bid off by Captain Rood at $2.25 per week, till March meeting. Mrs. Rogers was also bid off by him at $2.00 per week, if the selectmen cannot get her keep cheaper."

The hardships of those who were auctioned off were not necessarily less than for other paupers; for the lowest bidders were themselves very poor and merely sought added income. The abysmal living conditions of such boarding can well be imagined.

Another system for the local administration of poor relief was called the "outpension method." No institutionalizing was involved. It was relief given on a more or less temporary basis necessitated by some crisis, caused by accident or sickness, and it permitted the pauper or his family to stay put. The town records of West Windsor reveal an example. Dated July 20, 1889, they acknowledge payment of $8.00 "Received of F. S. Hale, Overseer of The Poor . . . as payment for care of Sam Oakes' family while she was insane. [Signed] J. E. Donahue." Another entry reads, "Bill for board of Will Spaulding. Board from Wed., Sept. 30th to Wed. Oct. 28th

$$4 \text{ weeks} - \$10.00$$
$$\underline{\text{credit for eggs} - .80}$$
$$\$ \ 9.20"$$

The record for Will Spaulding includes this note:

> Dr. Eastman: Don't think I told you that Will's hens have been stealing their nests since he has been building his hen house. I have found three nests in the grass and bushes. They were soiled and not saleable. I have taken them and allowed full prices for all the good ones.
>
> Ever,
>
> (Signed) V. Ely

Surely old Seth Chase never received such benevolent concern or treatment from his Overseer of the Poor. Otherwise his dread of the poorhouse would not have made him prefer starvation or freezing in the woods. Whatever was the cause of his death, the town paid "not more than" $75.00 for his funeral. That was the maximum rate. It included preparation, coffin, burial, and marker. The economics of old Seth Chase's life and death under the prevailing welfare system must include the footnote that J. R. Hill was paid $5.00 to varnish the town hearse.

A Rogues' Gallery of Vermont Counterfeiters

Part I

Well before our American Revolution, the way to make an easy buck was to print one's own. Judging by the widespread practice, the gains offset the risks. Counterfeiting was so extensive, according to historian Kenneth Scott, that in 1768 the *New York Journal* reported "they [the counterfeiters] have established a regular Chain of Communication through the whole Extent of the British Dominions in America, and that there are above an Hundred of them concerned in the different Provinces." The effect of such criminal enterprise was increased by the British themselves who later forged both the currencies of the separate states and of the Continental Congress in order to destroy the colonists' already precarious economy.

So concerned was Vermont's Assembly with the extent of counterfeiting that in 1779 it passed a law stipulating that anyone convicted of counterfeiting "should have his right ear cut off, should be branded on the forehead with a capital *C*, should forfeit his entire estate, and should be committed to the workhouse until the day of his death." To encourage the people's cooperation in bringing such criminals to justice, a bounty of ten pounds was offered. There is no record of how many rewards were paid. Yet the severity of the penalty proved to be no deterrent to the crime, as attested by the constant issuance of notices warning the public of bogus coins and bank notes. These warnings included instructions on how to detect the phony money. If severity of punishment was no deterrent, neither was leniency. In 1797 the Vermont legislature's amended statute against counterfeiting, which considerably lessened the harshness of punishment, noticeably failed to stem the tide of fake currency.

If counterfeiting was indeed "the first highly organized crime in America," surely Vermont's practitioners were among the most sophisticated, skillful, and numerous. Among the first to be apprehended (in December, 1789, for passing a bogus French guinea) was Peter Saunders, alias John Smith, who boasted he had "greatly deceived and taken in the inhabitants." *The Vermont Gazette* on February 8, 1790, declared that the rascal "alike prepared to act the saint and the villain, at one time preaches the gospel of Christ (as he says), with much vociferation and fervor, at the next with unsanctified hands, he distributes his counterfeits among the ignorant and unwary." In 1794 Pomfret's Seth Hathaway passed counterfeit coins but escaped the grand jury's indictment. One year later Strafford's Lebe Beebe was found guilty of passing Spanish dollars. (Note the implied prevalence of foreign money. Our country was so new that confidence in its own currencies, which were first federally minted and printed at Philadelphia in 1792, had not yet prevailed.) Partners John Johnson and Nicholas Allen of Norwich used iron molds to mill Spanish dollars for which, in 1797, they paid the price of imprisonment.

In Woodstock, counterfeiting seems to have been a cottage industry. In 1799 its Sewall Osgood forfeited $500 bail when indicted for having passed homemade Spanish dollars. In 1800, Sampson Davis got "good Spanish dollars" from David Smith (a third Woodstock citizen) "with the understanding that he would repay him with a large number of counterfeits." Later (in 1807) Woodstock's Abiather Boyce, Thomas Kimball, John Miles, and Levi Roberts were found guilty of counterfeiting. Jabez Thomas, who had helped counterfeiter Abner Hayes to escape, was duly punished, also for having passed counterfeit bills. Nineteen years later the postmaster of Gilead, Illinois, wrote to Vermont's Windsor County clerk asking for the conviction records of Woodstock's counterfeiting gang, because information about two of them, Jabez Thomas and Levi Roberts, "may be of great use to the good People of this county and answer Publick Justice."

Shrewsbury townsmen Ephriam Wood and Appollos Finney were busy passing bogus bills until the latter was convicted. Two years later, in 1799, Thomas Robinson, a transient, was indicted for having circulated fake Bank of the United States $10 bills, but he escaped conviction by jumping bail. The three Crane brothers were accused of the flood of silver coins that circulated throughout the state about 1800. Their equipment, some of which was stolen from the Reuben Harmon mint that legitimately produced copper cents, had been hidden in Mt. Antone's woods near Shrewsbury. Although the Crane brothers escaped, two were later said to have been hanged down south.

Despite the 1797 revision of penalties for counterfeiting that thereafter included "being set in the pillory, cropping of one or both ears and paying a fine," by 1802 Vermonters were victimized by an increasing deluge of counterfeit coins and bills. From 1802 to 1809, in Caledonia County, sixty indictments for counterfeiting or passing were made; whereas in 1808 alone, a check in seven counties revealed there were sixty-three indictments for counterfeiting or "uttering [circulating] base money." Yet the majority escaped punishment because they either avoided capture, jumped bail, or escaped from jail. Some very likely made bail with counterfeit money and then disappeared, forfeiting the fruit of their felonious labor.

Much of the flood was attributed to the prodigious industry of Stephen Burroughs, an infamous rascal whose exploits he "celebrated" in his *Memoirs,* published in 1811. Born the only son of Hanover, New Hampshire's Presbyterian minister Eden Burroughs, he boasted "I became the terror of the people where I lived, and all were very unanimous in declaring that Stephen Burroughs was the worst boy in town." But he did not stay long. He disappeared, joined the army, deserted, then entered Dartmouth College from which he was expelled. On his return from a trip to France he briefly became a teacher. Earlier he had been a bogus minister named Davis, in Pelham, Massachusetts. As a preacher he enhanced his image with twelve sermons that he had stolen from his father. It was while he was a minister—perhaps he watched the Sunday collection being harvested—that he got the inspiration for counterfeiting as the true path to quick wealth. While still a minister, he joined two "coiners" until he was caught passing the counterfeits in Springfield, Massachusetts. He was then sentenced to be stood in the pillory, lashed, and to serve a three-year term in Northampton's jail. However, he had no taste for confinement. After he had attempted to escape by setting the building on fire, he was shipped to Boston's Castle Island where he was a chronic troublemaker.

On the completion of his sentence, he became a schoolmaster at Charleton, near Worcester. There he married his uncle's daughter, Sally Davis. Marriage also proved too confining, and affairs with two of his pupils, plus another female, caused his imprisonment in Worcester's jail, from which he escaped. He fled to Long Island where he resumed teaching, presumably as a cover for his nefarious pursuits; when his prospects soured, he deserted his wife and children and went south.

In 1797 he had returned to his father's Hanover farm. Farming neither replenished his purse nor cleansed his soul. It merely fertilized his ambition for money. Further troubles prompted him to flee to Canada in 1799. His *Memoirs* revealed that Stephen Burroughs had been jailed both in Quebec City and Montreal for counterfeiting. In 1804, according to his book, he managed a farm and mills elsewhere in Canada. The mills, of course, were his counterfeiting operations, as so many defrauded Vermonters were to discover.

A confederate of Mr. Burroughs, Samuel Spring, was jailed in 1805 for passing bogus bills in Barre. Sheriff Micah Barron had produced evidence of fourteen $5 and sixty-five $10 bills. The dragnet also caught three of Spring's bona fide accomplices: John St. Clair, John Giles, and Russell Underwood of Putney. They were duly convicted and jailed. Yet seven other syndicate members had jumped bail. Flushed with his successful haul and armed with Canada's consent and cooperation, Sheriff Barron had Stephen Burroughs arrested and jailed in Montreal, for some of his handiwork had been fobbed off on Canadians.

Burroughs with his confederates had made Canada a large and lucrative source of counterfeit money, even while he was in jail.

Such respites were brief. By December of 1806 he had fled his Montreal jail with the aid of counterfeit keys. Arrests continued. In the shop and house of Springfield's Francis McAllister, three counterfeiters were seized (one of whom was fresh from the Canadian connection), and with them such evidence as plates, paper, a rolling press, and a quantity of bogus money. In early 1807 an accomplice of Burroughs named Remington, who had previously been indicted in Montreal, plus three cohorts named Allen, Mix, and Winslow, were seized in Shrewsbury. While out on bail, Allen and Remington were re-arrested for having counterfeited United States Bank notes. In April, Burroughs emerged again, this time in isolated Shipton and, according to an item in *The Weekly Wanderer,* the Peacham, Vermont, journal, "was daily emitting bills." The account related that, alerted by his emissaries, he had escaped the posse by a scant fifteen minutes. However, his press, plates, ink, and other supplies were destroyed.

One August day in 1807, South Hero's resident counterfeiter, Samuel Plumb, escaped in Vergennes from the custody of Grand Isle County's bailiff and sheriff. Vermont authorities were so incensed by the flood of bogus money that the *Burlington Sentinel* on January 6, 1808, reported that an example to other counterfeiters was made in the punishment given to Silas Whitney, "an old transgressor, who was sentenced to receive thirty-nine stripes, stand one hour in the pillory, pay a fine of three hundred dollars, and be confined to hard labor for five years." Two juvenile accomplices also received thirty-nine lashes but were spared a jail term.

Meanwhile, back in Canada, (according to a July 27, 1810, item in the *Vermont Sentinel)* "the notorious Stephen Burroughs was lately sentenced to transportation from Canada to Botany Bay [Great Britain's prison colony in Australia] . . . but was afterwards pardoned on giving heavy [presumably non-counterfeit] bonds for his future good conduct. On the condemnation of this ringleader of iniquity all his confederates suddenly decamped, & it is supposed are now returned to the United States."

Stephen Burroughs was then forty-five. Yet his additional thirty years of life are strangely unaccounted for. Could such anonymity mean that this compulsive, boastful mischief-maker with a proven record as a counterfeiter had assumed the guise of a devoted family man, once again in the disguise of a minister or teacher? In short, had Stephen Burroughs finally made of himself the successful counterfeit of a normal, law-abiding citizen?

Part II

Psychiatrists might attribute Castleton's Elijah Remington's career as a counterfeiter to the fact that he was a counterfeit himself. For in 1783 he was christened with the name of his dead half-brother. His father, tavern owner Zadock Remington, was Castleton's most zealous Tory, for which the state confiscated his property. He eventually was permitted to repossess through purchase a portion of his former holdings. Yet his fortunes ebbed and flowed on the tides of his questionable ethics, and Elijah was nourished on the milk of his father's bitterness.

Elijah's first arrest for counterfeiting was made in Montreal. Three years later, in 1807, at twenty-seven, he was nabbed in Shrewsbury, Vermont, while he was an accomplice of the infamous imposter and counterfeiter Stephen Burroughs; Elijah was sentenced to serve ten years in the Vermont State Prison at Windsor. Yet Castleton claimed him as its own, for there he had been born; there the townspeople—twice—petitioned the court to pardon the black-sheep son of their irascible but colorful tavern-keeper.

His pardon appeal was supported by a petition signed by ninety-seven Castleton citizens. However, the Governor's Council rejected it, despite his plea that, although the trial was fair, his wife and little ones were suffering great privation, and that he was determined to live "an honest and inoffensive life" if he were restored "to the liberty which by folly and wickedness I have so justly forfeited." A second petition was signed by 193 Castletonians, including four clergymen, two lawyers, mill owners, and a pewterer. After the board of prison visitors had added their endorsement, the Governor's Council granted Elijah Remington his pardon.

Thirteen years later the good people of Castleton found their trust in Elijah had been ill-founded. He resided in the county jail for nineteen months on a conviction of adultery. He could neither post bail nor pay the two hundred dollar fine plus costs. This time, however, even the warden joined his Castleton friends. So the Council suspended the fine and released forty-three-year-old Elijah Remington who, destitute, judiciously disappeared to the relief of his well-wishers.

The five ingredients for a flourishing counterfeiting operation were: a skilled engraver and/or die-maker, a printer with an efficient press, ample high-grade supplies (such as paper, inks, molds, etc.), and a contact man whose dual functions were to acquire—usually by theft—bills and coins to be counterfeited or kited (the raising of numerals), and to pass the bogus money in busy, previously untainted territory. Transcending all these was the fifth ingredient: luck.

The careers of two notorious counterfeiting partners, Christian Meadows, alias Martin Williams, and William Warburton, alias Bristol Bill, reveal that luck was indeed the fickle mistress of fortune. The Vermont State Prison at Windsor was host to both men.

Prisoner No. 1,348, with the preposterous Christian name of Christian, had served an earlier term for feloniously practicing his expertise as one of New England's foremost engravers. Christian Meadows had begun his counterfeiting activities in January, 1849, when he had stolen dies and banknotes from his Boston employer, W. W. Wilson, for whom he worked as an engraver. It was then that, as Martin Williams, he became the accomplice of William Warburton, alias Bristol Bill. They were identified by the cashier of the bank at Wells River, which they had robbed, and were trailed to Groton, Vermont, and arrested there in March, 1849, by Colonel Jacob Kent, the county sheriff. Among the evidence seized at the Groton house of Ephriam Low were the "one hundred thirty-five dies of bank names and bank note vignettes which have been stolen from Wilson." It was thus that Christian Meadows was an inmate at the state prison from June 22, 1850, to July 4, 1853. So outstanding was his craftsmanship that, while still confined, he was commissioned to do an official view of Dartmouth College. The superintendent assigned Meadows a guard for the trips to Hanover to do the drawings.

Another commission was directly responsible for his winning

freedom. It was an engraving for a diploma for the New Hampshire
State Society for the Advancement of Agriculture, Manufactures,
Science and the Arts that featured an elm tree identified as "the
Webster Elm that grew beside the great man's birthplace at
Franklin." This tree was responsible for Christian Meadows being
pardoned by Vermont's governor. A copy of the diploma had
been sent to Daniel Webster who was then President Fillmore's
Secretary of State. Mr. Webster was so pleased with the etching
that on learning the engraver was a prisoner he chided, "Why do
you bury your best talents in your state prisons?" Mr. Webster
wanted to give Christian Meadows employment at the State Department to engrave some maps.

In 1851 Daniel Webster wrote to Vermont's Governor Charles
Williams requesting that Meadows be pardoned. The request was
denied. The governor explained that because the prisoner was
serving his second term for larceny and counterfeiting of federal
currency a pardon was not warranted. Two years later, however,
Governor Erastus Fairbanks discovered his predecessor's corre-
spondence and freed Christian Meadows on July 4, 1853. He not
only journeyed to Windsor to present the pardon himself, but
"contributed $100 toward the purchase of a new house in
Windsor." The house, which also became his studio, was diagonally
across the street from the jail. It was here that Meadows did a
number of famous engravings: one of The Pavilion House hotel
at Montpelier, now a state office building, and the museum and
library of the Vermont Historical Society; and another of The
Windsor House that for many years decorated that historic hotel's
letterhead.

Daniel Webster's death in October, 1852, denied Meadows the
position of official engraver at the State Department. But he
prospered from his etching commissions, some of which were
portraits. He also engraved silver for Woodstock's Roswell H.
Bailey and other silversmiths, and embellished firearms for various
Vermont manufacturers.

There is no evidence that Martin Williams, ne Christian Meadows, had resumed his association with the infamous bank robber
and counterfeiter, William Warburton. For one thing, Warburton
was still in involuntary residence across the street, and presumably

Top: Die for counterfeit coin by Christian Meadows.
Bottom: Etching of Dartmouth College by Christian Meadows.

Christian Meadows was now smart enough to exploit his engraving skill legitimately rather than to jeopardize his good luck.

The adventures of William Warburton, alias Bristol Bill, is a case history of the vagaries of luck. The notorious criminal was born in Great Britain. It was said that he arrived in America as an escapee from Britain's Botany Bay prison colony in Australia, and that he had earned his alias for having made a considerable haul from a Bristol, Rhode Island, bank.

Bristol Bill next emerged as one of the ringleaders of a counterfeiting gang headquartered in Groton, a small, remote Vermont village. The discovery was made by Christian Meadows's former Boston employer, Mr. Wilson. After a two-year search, and mostly by luck, Mr. Wilson (who had the obsessive tenacity of Victor Hugo's Police Inspector Javert) had traced Meadows to Wells River. There he learned from the Wells River Bank's cashier, a Mr. Hale, that a suspicious character with the signature "W. H. Warburton, of Groton," had been in town for some months. From a description of the man, Mr. Wilson suspected that he was indeed Bristol Bill.

His pursuit of Meadows led him to Groton. There a posse was convened, and on the night of March 12, 1850, they raided the farmhouse of Ephriam Low, a once highly regarded Groton citizen who proved to have been the instigator of the "Groton Bank gang." The raid netted Low and Bristol Bill, along with his roommate Margaret O'Connell, a fetching Boston counterfeiter and "front." The dragnet included the mysterious Martin Williams (Christian Meadows) who lived nearby with his wife and child; also McLean Marshall, "English Jim" (a bank-robbing partner of Bristol Bill's), and Peter M. Paul.

The gang was arraigned on March 19. The trial was held in June at Danville's Caledonia County Court. While the case was before the grand jury, New Yorkers Samuel Drury, senior and junior, were arrested as accomplices for having in their possession "large sums of fraudulent, false and counterfeit bills," according to the indictment, that duplicated those issued by four banks in three states, including the burglarized Bristol, Rhode Island bank.

Bristol Bill was tried and found guilty of three of four indictments involving burglary, possession of burglary tools, felonious intent, etc. However, before sentences were imposed, his Boston lawyers challenged the verdict by filing a Bill of Exception. Thus the Supreme Court was to hear the case at Danville that August.

Two days after his guilty verdict for burglary, Bristol Bill returned to court to face counterfeiting charges along with Christian Meadows. Their defense lawyers were horrified to learn that State's Attorney Bliss M. Davis was to have their clients' accomplices, Peter M. Paul and McLean Marshall, testify for the prosecution as state's evidence. They did. The defense collapsed. Each defendant was sentenced to hard labor for ten years in the State Prison at Windsor.

Only by a fluke of miraculous luck did State's Attorney Davis survive the trial. For the verdict so enraged Bristol Bill that when Mr. Davis had bent over to commiserate with the badly stricken Meadows, Bristol Bill, who was shackled but not handcuffed, sprang at the prosecutor and drove a knife to its hilt into his neck and yelled, "Take that and if I could kill Marshall too, I'd be willing to hang!" A court officer yanked the blade free. It had just missed the jugular vein. Mr. Davis recovered.

After Mr. Meadows's petition for a pardon was granted in 1853, Bristol Bill asked Governor Stephen Royce to consider his own release. The request was referred to State's Attorney Davis. It was answered by Mr. Davis's wife in her husband's absence. In her letter of disapproval, Mrs. Davis reminded him that at heart he was a murderer, that only a fraction of an inch had saved her eight children from being orphans and she a widow.

In June of 1855, Bristol Bill was tried for assault with intent to kill. Before the trial, however, he had written to Mrs. Davis begging for her forgiveness, mercy, and for her intercession with Governor Royce. He protested that at heart he was a kind fellow with a nice disposition who was "so obliging to all . . . that even his enemies loved him." He invited her to visit him at the jail so she could assure herself how sorry he was and how sincere. She wrote to decline the visit, but said that she had forgiven him.

With the verdict of guilty, Bristol Bill was given seven additional years at hard labor. According to the *Caledonian-Record,* a St. Johnsbury, Vermont, newspaper, on June 11, 1856, only four days after the trial, Bristol Bill was pardoned by Governor Royce. With such luck it is reasonable to suppose that bank robber and counterfeiter William Warburton, alias Bristol Bill, abided by the terms of his pardon; namely that he quit the state forthwith and never set foot—or hand—in Vermont again.

Windsor's Slave-Owning Judge

In Windsor's Old South churchyard is a tombstone inscribed:

In Memory of
One of the Fathers of the
State of Vermont:
Hon. Stephen Jacob:
For many years
An eminent Councellor and an upright
Judge.
A distinguished Citizen, a benevolent
Neighbor, And an honest man:
Who departed this life
In the hope of a happy immortality
27 Jany. A.D. 1816
in the 61 year of his age.
Blessed are the Peacemakers for they
shall be called the children of God

Actually Judge Stephen Jacob had died a year later. Perhaps the engraver's error reflected the community's eagerness to put to rest the scandal that sullied the reputation of the none-too-

Honorable Judge Jacob. The date was a minor mistake considering the gravity of three other errors. For the following fact and
its consequences revealed him not to have been "an upright
Judge" nor "a benevolent neighbor" nor "an honest man."

On July 26, 1783, Jotham White of Charlestown, New Hampshire, "did sell and deliver" a Negro woman slave named Dinah
to Stephen Jacob, Esq. of Windsor, Vermont. The price paid for
the thirty-year-old slave was forty pounds. The contract of sale
was duly witnessed and recorded.

Note that the bill of sale for the slave woman was made six
years after Vermont's Constitution of 1777 explicitly prohibited
slavery. Judge Jacob was not Vermont's only slave owner. Despite its constitutional prohibition, slavery existed to a degree that
prompted a Vermont legislative enactment in 1786 of a law pro-
hibiting the sale and transportation of Negroes. The law added,
"the idea of slavery is expressly and totally exploded from our
free government."

After he had graduated from Yale in 1778, Stephen Jacob
opened his law office in Windsor. As was—and is—customary, he
swore to honor and uphold the state's constitution. Known as
the Oath of Allegiance, it was a pledge he had repeated at his in-
duction to each of the numerous governmental and judicial offices
he held, including his appointment to the State Supreme Court.
Yet the fact of Dinah's servitude violated the law of the state he
had so often sworn to uphold. But he was not impeached.

However, he was sued; sued by the Town of Windsor's selectmen, not for having owned a slave woman in violation of the law,
although that was particularly reprehensible to Windsorites. After
all, its Old Constitution House, now a museum, had been host to
those delegates whose abhorrence of slavery compelled them to
outlaw it. For Vermont was militantly abolitionist. So much so
that her courts often defied the Federal Fugitive Slave Law by
following Supreme Court Judge Theophilus Harrington's famous
precedent. In a case involving the surrender of a captured fugitive,
the good judge declared that the slave's owner had failed to prove
title to the man by not having shown "a bill of sale from Almighty
God." Instead, Judge Jacob was sued because Windsor was obliged
to provide the slave woman with medical care and lodging after

he had turned her out "sometime in 1800 when she became infirm, sick and blind." The suit sought to hold Judge Jacob responsible for her support, claiming that was not the town's obligation.

Windsor had a formidable adversary. The young lawyer had distinguished himself as a poet at the Battle of Bennington's first anniversary. He served several terms as Windsor's representative to the General Assembly. He then was elected a member of the Council of Censors in 1785. A year later he was the state's attorney for Windsor County, and was praised for his courage and leadership in quelling the Hartland insurrection.* Three years later Stephen Jacob was appointed one of Vermont's commissioners to arbitrate the settlement of a long-standing feud with New York. Then, after Vermont had joined the Union in 1791, President Washington appointed him the first United States district attorney for the district of Vermont. He was also the Windsor County Court's chief judge, as well as on the Governor's Council from 1796 to 1801. The next three years Stephen Jacob was a member of the Vermont Supreme Court.

His contributions to both his community and state were undeniably impressive. In the *Vermont Journal* of January 16, 1892, Judge Russell Taft's mostly laudatory biographical profile included these other commitments: Stephen Jacob was Windsor's town moderator for 1786, a school trustee, selectman, and lister. For many years he was a trustee of the Dartmouth College Corporation, and a one-time master of Windsor's Masonic Lodge. He gave the state the land on which to build the State Prison. The acreage was almost directly opposite his elegant State Street mansion. "His hospitality was unbounded, his benevolence proverbial. . . . In his domestic establishment he kept many servants, some of whom

---

* In the fall of 1786 a mob from Hartland and Barnard tried to disrupt a session of Windsor's county court to protest a jurisdictional decision. The mob was dispersed; their leaders were tried, fined, and imprisoned, "Soon after, about 50 of the insurgents, under arms, assembled in Hartland to rescue those in prison. The militia were called out, the rioters attacked, and twenty-seven captured. Mr. Jacob was wounded in the melee. The rioters were subsequently punished." (From the *Vermont Journal*, January 16, 1892.)

were colored slaves (purchased by him and brought into the state, where they were free to go and come at their own pleasure)," declared Judge Taft. However, that is not to say that they were freed from bondage.

Another reference to Judge Jacob appeared in Jacob Ullery's *Men of Vermont*. "Judge Jacob," he wrote, "was a high-strung Federalist and of aristocratic bearing." The article also reported that "he bought several slaves and brought them to Vermont, but that since slavery was prohibited by the Vermont Constitution, the so-called slaves were free to leave at will." Yet there is no record that Judge Jacob ever gave Dinah her freedom. On the contrary, eighteen years after her purchase, and of his own free will, he boldly confirmed his ownership of the slave woman by his July, 1801, amendment, affixed to the original contract of sale. The endorsement stated: "I certify that the foregoing is a true copy of a bill of sale executed to me by Jotham White, Esq. and consent that the same use of this copy should be made in Court as might be of the original Instrument.[signed] Stephen Jacob." Nor did he deny the validity of these documents at either of his two trials. Instead, at the first trial he astutely had them declared irrelevant and therefore inadmissible. Ullery might have added that Judge Jacob was shrewd, wily, and arrogant, as his defense proved.

The plaintiffs were Windsor's selectmen, for they were also the town's overseers of the poor. They sought a judgment against Judge Jacob because a slave owner was liable for the support of his slave and could not turn the slave upon the town to be supported by the public. In addition to recovering what the slave's support had cost the town, Windsor was also seeking "the further sum of one hundred dollars for work, labor, care and diligence."

Judge Jacob denied the allegations, stated he wished to stand trial, and filed for "a plea in abatement," which is a request for a reduction of charges and/or a decrease of damages sought.

The plaintiffs' premise was that, as overseers of the poor, they were duty-bound to support out of the public funds paupers "legally residing in the town." Town officers were authorized by statutes to "evict persons likely to become public charges, provided such persons were legally warned to depart before acquiring a legal residence." Surely Dinah had received no such warning on the assumption that as Judge Jacob's servant she would not "come to want." An even more crucial point was the question raised by the defense: Was Dinah legally a resident, being illegally possessed as a slave?

The case of *Selectmen of Windsor* v. *Stephen Jacob* came to trial in March, 1801, at the County Court at Woodstock. Judge Jacob was at that time its chief judge. He chose not to disqualify himself from presiding as judge at his own trial. His assistant judges, both colleagues, were Jesse Williams and Elizah Robinson. Neither one objected. No jury was impaneled. The defendant's plea in abatement contended "that the action brought by the selectmen was brought in behalf of the inhabitants of Windsor, that the summons had been served on the defendant by Stephen Conant, deputy sheriff, and therefore virtually one of the plaintiffs, and that a summons could not legally be served by one of the parties plaintiff. This plea was considered by the court to be sufficient and it was adjudged that the writ abate and that *the defendant be allowed costs against the plaintiffs* (italics added) in the sum of four dollars and seventy-five cents."

The plaintiffs appealed to the Vermont Supreme Court. The case was docketed for August, 1801. Judge Jacob applied for a continuance which was granted. A year later, in August, the case came to trial. Postponements were even then a popular delaying action for defendants. This time, however, Judge Jacob, who had been elevated to the State Supreme Court, did not join his colleagues on the bench. The case was tried *de novo* (anew, from the beginning). The plea in abatement by which Judge Jacob had won in the lower court was either not sought or, if it had been, it was summarily overruled. This time a jury was impaneled. The selectmen's attorney, a Mr. Hubbard, established Judge Jacob's ownership of Dinah with the evidence of Jotham White's bill of sale to the defendant. The defendant's attorney, a Mr. Marsh, objected, claiming that because no one could legally be a slave in Vermont, the paper was inadmissible. Mr. Hubbard needed to establish the fact of Dinah's ownership to assert Judge Jacob's obligation for her support. The point was crucial. So attorney Hubbard adroitly conceded, stating, however, "that if a master will hold an African in bondage as a slave *contrary to right*, and for a succession of years, during which the slave *de facto* spends the vigor of her life in service . . . there is a moral obligation to support her when incapable of labor; and the law of common justice, upon which all equitable actions are founded, will imply a promise in him to respond any necessary expenses incurred by others for her support."

Mr. Marsh was eager to put Judge Jacob in a more favorable light with a statement that would blunt the legal argument. It was an eloquent speech. The court made no objection to it despite the fact that it "could hardly be described as relevant to the question whether the bill of sale should, or should not be admitted in evidence." Mr. Marsh declared: "Some time in the year 1783, the defendant brought the woman Dinah into this State. She continued in his family several years; and there can be but little doubt, from the excellent character and disposition of her master, she would have so continued until this time in sickness and in health; but several of the inhabitants of Windsor . . . discovering that she was an excellent servant, and wishing to profit themselves of her labours, inveigled her from her master's service by the siren songs of liberty and equality, which have too often turned wiser heads. She spent the vigor of her life with these people and wasted her strength in their service; and now she is blind, paralytic, and incapable of labour, they aim by this suit to compel the defendant *solely* to maintain her.

"When she was enticed from the defendant's service, he did not attempt to reclaim her. As an inhabitant of the State, in obedience to the constitution, he considered that he could not hold her as a slave. Is it equitable then, that when the sovereign power had dissolved the tenure by which he held her services, and when he had been deprived of her labours by the enticement of others . . . he should now be compelled to maintain her in the decrepitancy of old age?"

Defense attorney Marsh ended his argument with what is nowadays called "doublespeak." He declared that Judge Jacob was under no obligation to support the slave woman "unless she had been *legally* his slave." But because Vermont's constitution outlawed slavery within its borders, no bill of sale could be a legal sanction for such ownership.

Judge Royall Tyler echoed the same refrain in voicing the court's judgment. He said: "The question must turn upon the validity or operating force of this instrument within this state. If the bill of sale could by our constitution operate to bind the woman in slavery when brought by the defendant to inhabit within this State, then it ought to be admitted in evidence; and the law will raise a liability in the slaveholder to maintain her through all the vicissitudes of life; but if otherwise it is void." With the bill of sale thus declared inadmissible, the plaintiffs were denied proof of Judge Jacob's ownership of Dinah, and Windsor's suit was lost. The selectmen were assessed fourteen dollars and seventy-five cents for court costs.

A year after the trial, Judge Jacob was not re-elected to the legislature, nor did he thereafter hold any public office. However, Judge Russell Taft attributed Judge Jacob's withdrawal from public life to political partisanship rather than to public censure for his ownership and treatment of Dinah. Alone and blind, she died on March 6, 1809; age, fifty-six.

The Borderline Crime

Often in history cause and effect are determined by the vagaries of disparate circumstances. Thus what made smuggling a major industry in landlocked Vermont can be ascribed to an incident on the high seas in June, 1807.

Two years earlier Britain's war with France had reached a stand-off. Napoleon's victory at Austerlitz had secured France's domination of the continent; whereas Nelson's victory at Trafalgar had given England supremacy on the seas. However, supremacy did not mean monopoly, not to the Americans. As a neutral nation they did not want their commerce with either side restricted. To thwart America's trading with France, Britain's capricious Orders-in-Council decreed her "right" to board and search American vessels. This insulting practice resulted in confiscations and the impressing—or involuntary recruitment—of American seamen.

On that spring day in 1807 the British warship, the *Leopard*, attacked the U. S. frigate *Chesapeake*. Three of the *Chesapeake's* crew were killed, eighteen were wounded, and four "alleged British deserters" were removed.

The outrage, a prelude to the War of 1812, was redressed by President Thomas Jefferson who had convened Congress in a special session to impose the Embargo Act. It was erroneously believed that restricting the merchant marine and thus denying

American provisions to the belligerents would guarantee American neutrality.

The Embargo Act was to boomerang. At first it did not faze landlocked Vermonters. They chose to believe that it only applied to commerce on the high seas. This interpretation, shared by local customs officers, permitted the usual overland transit of goods to Canada. The independent-minded Vermonters even excluded lumber rafts from the embargo. The rest of New England, however, was incensed by the Act, because so much of its economy depended on its maritime trade.

Vermonters enjoyed the popular jest that "embargo" spelled backward became "O-grab-me." They became accomplished and diligent "grabbers" themselves after March 12, 1808, when Congress strengthened the embargo with its supplementary "Land Embargo." It prohibited the exporting "in any manner whatever [of] any goods, wares, or merchandise." By the time the ink had dried, smuggling had become a northern Vermont industry.

The measure incited such an explosion of protest that Vermont's collector of customs, Jabez Penniman, wrote to Secretary of the Treasury Albert Gallatin advising him that any federal interference with the profitable rafting of lumber for the Canadian trade and the regular commerce of other cargoes would require the government to send troops to enforce the law. The message smacked of insurrection. Jefferson was alarmed. After he had consulted with Vermont's Senator Jonathan Robinson and Congressman James Witherell, Jefferson was determined that, if necessary, he would use force. If enforced, the embargo would be ruinous to Vermonters. Heated protest meetings were held in Burlington, Castleton, Milton, North Hero, and Shelburne.

It was ironic that rather than impoverish those who were engaged in Canadian trade, the embargo considerably enriched them. Because by smuggling, they no longer paid customs duties. Perhaps it was just such a war profiteer who used ridicule instead of vitriol to oppose the embargo. He wrote in the *Vermont Sentinel* in 1808, "This fag end of the Embargo goes to prohibit the farmers of Vermont . . . from driving their swine to Canada for sale. Now suppose a man should drive a herd of hogs close to the line of the United States, *but not over,* and a Canadian should ac-

cidentally make his appearance just within the boundry of that
British colony, with a basket of corn in his hand and should cry
Pig-Pig-Pig and the hole drove should run over the line into Canada,
and *voluntarily* place themselves under the government of the
tyrant of the ocean, who should be punished, the farmer who
drove his hogs so near despotism, the swine, who regardless of the
blessings of a free country, thus ran over the line, or the Canadian
who tempted them to this anti-republican act?"

More serious protests echoed Burlington's sentiments at town
meetings throughout the Champlain valley. St. Albans citizens,
riled by Jefferson's having accused protesters of treasonous conduct, proclaimed themselves "true and faithful citizens," but insisted that the duty of good citizenship required that "individuals
finding themselves and their families on the verge of ruin and
wretchedness . . . evade the embargo restrictions." They were of
one mind in proclaiming that their obligation "as *free and independent Republicans was* . . . to examine the measures of government." Such talk was the rhetoric of secession. Its rebellious echo
resounded throughout Vermont in the traditional spate of Fourth
of July oratory.

Chief Customs Collector Penniman promptly sought help to
impose what he called "the loathsome restrictions." He had
deputized local enforcers. That failing, they were replaced by the
militia. Governor Israel Smith ordered a 150-man detachment of
Franklin County's brigade to Alburg's Windmill Point where they
were to stop the transit of lumber rafts. Because some of the men's
loyalty was to the raftsmen, many of whom were neighbors or
acquaintances, half of the unit was replaced by a 150-man detachment of Rutland County's militia. Sixteen regular cannons plus
two brass six-pounders augmented the force.

Suspicion of the militia's impotence was justified. The *Vermont
Sentinel* periodically published the number of desertions. A John
Henry reported "the militia men refused to fire on those who
were passing in contempt of the law, and a few prisoners whom
they seized were immediately released from an apprehension of a
rescue by the inhabitants." The more widespread the smuggling
became, the more prevalent were rumors of the enforcers' failures.

Rumors made good copy. The *Vermont Sentinel* claimed that

"an armed force of ninety men in disguise" brought a raft to Canada with "little opposition." Another raft, reported to be "nearly half a mile long," loaded with "wheat, potash, pork, beef, etc., worth more than $3000," was identified as having "a regular fort built upon it ball proof, and . . . manned with between 5 and 600 armed men."

Customs Chief Jabez Penniman knew that smuggling was so common that the reports in the *Vermont Sentinel* and other papers were merely isolated, magnified views of a far greater reality. With tenacity he redoubled his efforts to stop the illegal traffic. He had bought and outfitted a cutter to blockade Lake Champlain's outlet at Windmill Point. But smugglers captured it and added it to their outlawed flotilla.

By another aborted effort, Penniman became an unwitting accomplice to a nearly successful smuggler. The man's name was Samuel Mott. He was one of the thugs whom Penniman had hired to flush out smugglers for his fellow revenuers. Samuel Mott's scheme was to sell seized contraband for his own profit. He was discovered. Later he boasted that he had only joined Penniman's little fleet to have all the other smugglers apprehended, to have his boat armed, and then he "could do the business of the Lake," which was what he did, and which undid him.

Penniman had posted Mott aboard a revenue cutter that patrolled Lake Champlain's Missisquoi Bay area, one of the smugglers' favorite landfalls. The fact that much of the bay was Canadian territory compounded Penniman's surveillance problems. Near there in the Winooski River one August day in 1808, *The Fly* captured the notorious smugglers' vessel, *The Black Snake.* It was a forty-foot, tar-coated row galley owned by a St. Albans merchant. In the engagement, *The Fly's* captain, David Farrington, was badly wounded, and three crew members lost their lives. *The Black Snake's* skipper, William Mudgett, was hanged. The others were given long prison terms. But so tolerant of smuggling were north country citizens that the guilty were soon pardoned. No fine was imposed on the ship's owner.

Despite Mott's perfidy, between May and October, Penniman and his New York counterpart, Melancton Wolsey, captured over twelve ships. Their cargoes of butter, leather, tea, and more than three hundred barrels of ash were seized. Prior to their sale by auction, the confiscated goods were stored in privately owned warehouses. Greed was not limited to the smugglers. Customs officers "profited handsomely from their seizures and even charged the United States government for storing confiscated ashes," according to a newspaper account.

Smugglers had predators besides those voracious revenue agents. They were informants who tipped off customs officials to an expected shipment of contraband from or into Canada and were rewarded with one-third the value of the seized goods. It was a profitable enterprise involving no investment, little risk of vengeance, but much resentment. Although most of the provisions were seized by customs officers in border towns, they made hauls throughout all of northern Vermont, including Alburg, Burlington, Cambridge, Coventry, Fairfax, Georgia, Highgate, Johnson, Milton, Newport, North Hero, St. Albans, Swanton, Underhill, and some fifteen other towns.

War profiteering was endemic. Farmers with large herds of cattle got triple the cost of beef before the hostilities between France and England. In the Champlain valley war profiteers had a thriving business supplying the enemy's forces with beef and pork even while the enemy was devastating Vermont's northern borders. In May lumbermen sent their rafts north on Lake Champlain on their annual spring shipments. Even American troops, often as members of local militias, were known to help smugglers get their produce over the border, or they turned their backs on the traffic, or gave the smugglers competition by themselves engaging in illicit trade.

Smugglers formed combines. One such syndicate, known as the Catlin gang, consisted of Burlington's Moses and Guy Catlin, Gideon King, and a mysterious Spaniard named Ramon Manzuco. The group even included the intelligence services of C. P. Van Ness, another customs collector for Vermont. One of their best customers was John Jacob Astor. In addition to buying and selling furs, English manufactured goods, and Vermont produce, the Catlin gang acted as commission agents for others. From Canada, English and Canadian goods passed through Swanton and Burlington thence throughout upper New York State and also to Boston.

Ramon Manzuco's Spanish citizenship made him a valuable member of the gang. Because the Burlington resident was a "neutral," he skippered Gideon King's 50-ton sloop, the *Saucy Fox,* under the Spanish flag which kept it immune from search and seizure.

Commodities in greatest demand, and therefore most profitable for the smugglers, were livestock, dressed meat and hides, tea, potash and pearlash, and lumber. Furs were exempt from the embargo, perhaps because fur-trader John Jacob Astor wielded so much influence in Washington and Montreal or perhaps because the huge customs revenues accruing from Europe's great demand for pelts helped to replenish the U. S. Treasury's war chest. Astor shipped his goods with Gideon King, Burlington's notorious smuggler. Known as "the Admiral of Lake Champlain," he used Astor's tariff immunity to protect his contraband provisions.

The embargo's failure was evident even before the end of its first year. Relations with France as well as with Britain had worsened, so much so that the embargo nearly wiped out federal revenues. Finally official acknowledgment of the government's failure to check the epidemic lawlessness was made by Secretary of the Treasury Albert Gallatin, who was responsible for the embargo's enforcement. He had reported to Jefferson that "because the administration was not properly supported by the people . . . the stoppage of intercourse [was] so unpopular . . . that the revenue agents and other truly friendly characters are afraid to act."

Yet the greater the embargo's failure, the more repressive Congress became. Gallatin's insistence on even stiffer enforcement measures defeated a Congressional draft for the embargo's repeal. Another Enforcement Act was passed on January 9, 1809, after seven weeks of bitter debate. It empowered federal agents without warrants to confiscate all products that they suspected were destined for export, and held them immune from legal recourse. Jefferson personally endorsed the Act with a directive to all governors which demanded they provide sufficient militia to stop the smuggling.

Outrage reverberated throughout the Champlain valley. At meetings in Burlington, St. Albans, Swanton, Williston and as far south as Hartland, treasonous utterances were applauded. The hate was directed not against the British whose increasing harassment of American ships was responsible for the embargo and its Enforcement Act, but against Jefferson and Secretary of the Treasury Gallatin. Thus some of the hate was domestically incited. The embargo was the sledge hammer that drove a political wedge between Jefferson's Republicans and New England's Federalists. Yet when war against Britain was declared in 1812, a Republican majority in Vermont joined ranks with the federal government in a burst of loyalty that produced Vermont's own "non-importation" or embargo act. However, the act was soon ignored. For northern Vermonters, observance of the embargo acts would have spelled bankruptcy. While its violation meant survival, wholesale violation meant prosperity. Thus the declaration of war merely increased the smuggling trade, because Canada's British forces badly needed all the timber, beef, and other provisions that Vermonters were happy to supply. An enemy that was such a good customer was regarded more as an ally; whereas the American government, whose embargo—if enforced—could bankrupt them, was perceived as the enemy.

Resourcefulness was always Vermonters' strong suit. There were many smuggling ploys as devious as Samuel Mott's parasitic pickings. The craft of smuggling had become an art. One popular was to being goods into and from Canada was merely to leave the freight at remote or wooded border areas where after dark Canadian or Vermont accomplices would "steal" it. Alburg, Champlain, and Highgate were the destinations on the shipments' manifests. Another smugglers' thoroughfare was through Coventry and Newport (then named Duncansborough). Even though the customs officers were aware of the ploy, their vigilance was no match for the smugglers' advantage of nighttime and the sparsely patrolled border wilderness; the bribery of the embargo-enforcers was insurance against their interference. In the best tradition of Mott's duplicity, smugglers seized those goods which the customs officers had captured.

Smugglers resorted to piracy. John Baker operated as a commissioned privateer. His appropriately named *Lark,* a modest sailboat armed with three muskets, hovered off Lake Champlain's

Rouses Point, close to Canada's border. There it would overtake ships headed for Canada with their freight. Because international law protected cargoes seized "by an armed privateer," the *Lark* and its booty were immune from seizure by federal revenue officials. The cargoes were sold in Canada for a prearranged price by their original owners who received the money, less a percentage for Captain Baker.

Another more simple ploy was the construction of wharves which jutted out from the border, one side fronting the United States, the other fronting Canada. By unloading American vessels on the American (south) side, and reloading the cargoes on the wharf's north (Canadian) side, the transfer was safe from seizure by the United States customs officers. An even simpler way to thwart the revenuers was the theft of the revenue cutter at Windmill Point by outwitting its guards. The fact that such a theft occurred more than once suggests collusion. There were so many skirmishes between revenue agents and smugglers at Windmill Point that it was more widely known as "Hellgate."

The law of gravity defied the law of Congress. According to the *Vermont Sentinel* of May 27, 1808, smugglers hauled produce up hills on the border there. "On the top a slight building is erected, in which barrels, pipes, and other articles are deposited. The construction of the house is such that on the removal of a stone or piece of wood, the whole edifice with its contents immediately falls on the British territory, by which means although apparently accidental, the laws are evaded."

Cattle defied the law merely by walking across the border at wooded sections strewn with grain. Franklin County's little village of Georgia was the beginning of the grain trail. A route via Mount Mansfield was so well trafficked by livestock and other commodities going to and from Canada that the pass is known— even on today's maps—as Smugglers Notch.

One smuggling episode was a community project to outsmart a Captain Simonds. He had arrived in the town of Derby expressly to stop the selling of foodstuffs to the English in Canada. Derby farmers were enraged by outsiders poking their noses into their business, especially their illegal business. One day ambitious, young Captain Simonds strode into the general store, made snide comments about local lawlessness, and declared that he and his men would see that the smuggling ventures ceased. Derby's townsmen bristled. They'd show that uppity bloodhound how a little Vermont ingenuity would settle his hash!

A cold snap and fresh, heavy snowfall were ideal for the chore of hog butchering. Locally pork brought ten cents a pound. Across the border the British quartermasters would pay about twenty-five cents a pound. The problem was how to avoid Captain Simonds's men. One woman proposed a big sleighing party to the King's Arms Inn, just across the border. A delegation of women sought the captain's permission. He consented, provided that they take nothing over or back; not so much as a yard of ribbon was to enter the States. The group agreed. At dusk they started from Decker's Tavern. Inside the tavern barn they bundled up and settled down in a large hay-filled sleigh. A Dr. Fields drove. They headed north. Captain Simonds stopped the sleigh and inspected it in the waning light. The women laughed gaily and invited him to join them on their outing. He declined, stating that his duties made merrymaking impossible. He good-naturedly waved them on, and the sound of sleigh bells mingled with giggles. When they reached the King's Arms, only those bonneted passengers who had sat on the outside alighted. The others rode right into the inn's stables. There the unshawling and unbonneting of the other seemingly ladylike passengers revealed the carcasses of freshly butchered hogs. The ruse had worked so well that, although its perpetrators had pledged themselves to silence, word of how they had outsmarted Captain Simonds spread like milkweed seeds in a brisk wind. Thereafter, Captain Simonds declined all dinner invitations. He had no appetite for pork—or for humble crow either.

The close of the war ended the embargo. Yet the spark of lawlessness did not flicker out. Smuggling again flared 106 years later when the Eighteenth Amendment outlawed the sale, transportation, and consumption of alcoholic beverages. The peace of Lake Champlain was rent by the wake of rum-running fleets of high-powered motorboats operated by bootleggers who were members of organized crime syndicates. Overland the same routes that had been taken by "embargo-busters" were trafficked by vehicles starting from the Canadian border, then filtering through Vermont into the thirsty reaches well south of the border. Smuggling had become more specialized, more sophisticated, more dangerous.

The ingredients that had made smuggling a Vermont industry were greed, individualism, and a cantankerous assertion of independence. Defiance of authority was a reflex action to economic distress and political dissent. Thus Vermonters can be said to have emulated the ideal of truly democratic enterprise by having achieved—through smuggling—a free flow of goods.

The Legend of "Long-Gone" Pond

Unlike many legends, the story of "Long-Gone Pond" is as 100 percent-proof true as the rum Aaron Wilson, Sr., offered to his townsmen that beautiful yet fateful June day in 1810.

Aaron Wilson of Glover, Vermont, had a blacksmith shop and two mills on a branch of Barton River. Wheelwrights, carriage makers, barrelmakers, and woodworkers had also located here; for all depended on water from streams that originated in Mud Pond. But the water supply was unreliable. In spring the streams were often so torrential that they damaged the dams. Yet in mid-summer not enough water trickled down to turn a waterwheel. Water power was only assured for the three months from about April first to July fourth. The mill operators and their workers whose living depended on waterpower had to contend with the vagaries of the rains.

In 1810, when this story begins, there was a long, unseasonal, spring drought. The millers' and farmers' worries increased as the grain and logs piled up. One June day mill-owner Aaron Wilson and his son left their idle mills and spent the day exploring the acres of thickets and swale around Mud Pond. There they made an extraordinary discovery. The next day miller Wilson urged his customers and other discouraged townspeople to come to his mill to hear of his discovery, one which could affect their lives in ways that none could have anticipated, except a skeptical Sheffield native, James Jenness.

First Aaron baited their attention by reminding them of what they all knew. No grinding, no sawing, no machining could be done without waterpower and "we ain't got no water." Then he declared that he had an idea for a solution. It was logical. It was simple. If the town's able-bodied men would dig in with him, he promised to provide a keg of rum. Their curiosity was instantly whetted.

Excitedly, yet with the authority of his conviction, Aaron told them he and his boy had discovered that Long Pond's northern end "is less than forty rods [660 feet] from Mud Pond that's drier 'n dust." Long Pond, which he reminded his audience was full of water, lay about ninety feet higher than dry Mud Pond. So wasn't it reasonable to suppose—just suppose—that if they all pitched in with him to dig a ditch from higher Long Pond to bone-dry Mud Pond, what with the guarantee that water would run downhill, they'd soon be grinding, shaping, and sawing again? All they had to do was bring their own crowbars and shovels—and brawn. The rum, he repeated, was on him.

The enthusiasm was thunderous, except for skeptical James Jenness who was said to have warned, "If you used yer God-given brains, Aaron Wilson, you'd know you cain't meddle with God's will. If He'd intended Long Pond to drain north into Lake Memphremagog, 'stead of south for Champlain, He'd sure as hell of arranged it thata way. I'm agin' triflin' with nature!"

Citizen Jenness was a minority of two. The other was sawmill owner and farmer David Blodgett who whispered to Jenness, "Can't say I like the smell of this any more'n you. How're they fixin' to stop the water once it starts arunnin' down hill?" James Jenness merely shrugged.

A date for the project was agreed upon. Work crews were allocated and scheduled. Aaron had thought of everything. In addition to the rum, he provided tin horns, explaining "These is for you fellers that know the country up yonder, so when you get into the woods the day we'll commence our diggin', blow hard to help t'others find the way, 'cause it sure's thick up there." The horns were given to those who knew the territory: Silas Wheeler,

Spencer Chamberlain, Loring Frost, and a few more.

The horns, picks, shovels, crowbars, and brawn were put to use by sixty-one men and boys on June 6, 1810. What a memorable day it was for folks in that part of Vermont! The digging bee began before daybreak, for some had to come many miles, a few on horseback, through unmarked rocky ravines and nearly impenetrable thickets. Led by horn-blowing Aaron Wilson, Jr., Isaac Stokes and Loring Frost, the brigade of diggers reached the northern point of Long Pond before nine o'clock. There the excavating was to begin. It was an awesome undertaking.

Long Pond extended for a mile and a half. It was about half as wide, and measured over three hundred acres. Except for its shallow shore, its depth varied from fifty to one hundred feet. According to an engineer who earlier had surveyed the site, Long Pond contained not less than 1,000,988,000 gallons at 1500 feet above sea level.

Here the Lamoille River's headwaters rise and flow south into a fertile valley before pouring into Lake Champlain. All of its shore had a solid rock bed, except for one spot at the northern end where a gravel bank contained its waters. The bank's approximate height of a few feet extended to a slope of five rods (or twenty-seven and a half yards) before descending between eighty and one hundred feet into the valley. Mud Pond was at the bottom of this valley, the valley in which the placid little towns of Barton, Glover, and Greensboro were cradled.

The work crews wisely had chosen to start their digging in a shallow spot where the sandy soil gave little resistance despite a network of roots through which they chopped. Perhaps the promise of the rum also helped to make their digging progress so quickly that the canal to Mud Pond was finished by 10:45 A.M. The sweaty workers plodded up the slope, the better to admire their accomplishment while a few labored to break through the final barrier. Sand and gravel flew away, deepening the channel to let the water rush in. But the men struck a solid shalelike crust. Finally they broke through. Nothing happened! The water merely disappeared into the sandbed like the tide escaping the moat of a child's sand castle.

The men stared incredulously. Suddenly—with a swoosh—the

canal walls collapsed, suctioning three men into quicksand to their armpits. They were hauled out by their hair. Relief from their narrow escape erupted in laughter—until a boy, pointing, shrieked, "Look! Look at that there whirlpool!" He was pointing to a swirling, sudsy, greenish-brown turbulence that had broken Long Pond's placid blue surface. Only a few yards from shore, it churned "as if from a subterranean eruption," and while its swirling, counter-clockwise spiral widened as it gained momentum, massive logs disappeared into its voracious funnel.

To observe the maelstrom more closely many of the diggers descended to what they thought was the safety of a log raft dry-docked in a clump of cattails. No sooner had they jumped aboard than the entire shoreline quaked with an ominous rumble. The men turned to see the bank on which they had stood only minutes before split into an instant gorge. Just in time they scrambled from the rumbling shore to the safety of higher ground. For the ditch's bottom disappeared as the unearthly roar of a billion gallons of water plummeted into the valley.

Long Pond swept along the new canal into Mud Pond for a height of twenty-five feet above its normal level, slicing the hill into deep ravines, while carrying along trees and boulders.

After the inertia of shock, the men, seeing the danger to their families and homes from the raging flood, raced to alert the townspeople. Spencer Chamberlain finally reached Wilson's mill and bellowed the warning to take to the hills, that Long Pond was sweeping down on them. The air throbbed with the cataract's deafening roar, with the deep cannon-like report of tree trunks snapping off and being carried along. In the swirling debris, a panic-stricken horse was swept away. The cascade pulverized many buildings including Wilson's mill. So devastating was the damage that to this day no trace of the gristmill's machinery, not even its huge stone grinding wheels, have ever been found, though these relics have been hunted ever since that beautiful June day, in 1810, that had begun with such great promise.

When the flood had pounded into Glover, it tore up and flushed away an entire pine-forested plain, leveling it so flat, so smooth that it was later used for regimental parades. Today Glover's souvenir of the flood can be seen in the Universalist church's found-

"Long-Gone" Pond raging through Glover.

ation. For a boulder said to have been seven feet wide, eighteen feet long, weighing almost one hundred tons, had been swept more than a mile to near the village center. There masons used sledge hammers and wedges to split it up for the church's and other building foundations.

By 3:00 P.M., and with devastated Glover in its wake, the flood surged into Barton at a height of twelve feet above the main street. Scoffer David Blodgett, who had opposed the ditch-digging project, was plowing when the distant roar alerted him to the flood. He raced to salvage what he could of his mill, then fled with his family to safety. In addition to his buildings, all his cattle, pigs, sheep, and hens were swept away. Later miller-farmer Blodgett sued those responsible for the digging bee that had so disastrously released Long Pond's water. For two years the case languished on the court's docket of postponements. It never was tried.

The flood's effect on the townspeople ran the gamut from the heroic to the absurd. Solomon Dorr, who had been rendered fearless by shots of brandy, carried the alarm to a schoolhouse. The teacher quickly herded his children to a hill now festooned with other townspeople. One was "Old Granny" Gould. She watched the destruction while knitting as calmly yet as resolutely as Madame Defarge. Her husband, "Grampy" Gould, fretted about having had to abandon three milk pans he had set out on the kitchen table. It'd be plumb wasteful to lose such rich cream. The next day when the old couple re-entered their house they found mud a foot thick over everything, everything but the kitchen table which had floated to the ceiling and come down in a different place, but with nary a drop of milk spilled.

Seven hours after Long Pond had burst its confines, the flood's crest reached Lake Memphremagog. That is twenty-five miles away, north of what is now Newport, Vermont. Along its entire route it averaged a height of over six feet, and where the ravines were filled with debris it attained a seventy-foot high-water mark.

The entire valley was awash with many thousands of fish "flopping in the sun." It was said that "five tons of trout, salmon, and eels were picked up, and bushels of bass and sunfish were salvaged from the muddy ooze" to be salted, smoked, or pickled.

The aftermath of the flood is full of ironies. It was long be-

lieved that the land was now useless for farming, because so
much of it was gravel-crusted while the rest was buried under
mud so soft that it would not provide footing for beast or man.
In time, however, it dried out, and when a farmer bought a hundred acres of this wasteland at one dollar per acre, it yielded a
"rich crop of herdsgrass six feet tall" in less than three years. The
pasturage proved the valley to be among Vermont's most fertile
land.

Time also has changed the public's ridicule and contempt for
those despoilers of God's handiwork. At the one hundredth anniversary of the catastrophe, Glover's townspeople venerated the
diggers as heroes, for had not those valiant citizens—albeit unwill-
ingly—engineered a solution to a dangerous drought without the
loss of a single human being, and thereby enriched the valley's
farmland? On that June 6, 1910, celebration of their ancestors'
feat, the citizens unveiled a splendid granite marker on the site
of Long Pond, which—since the labors of Aaron Wilson and his
pioneering ditch-diggers—more accurately should be known as
Long-Gone Pond. But the town now refers to the site as Runaway
Pond, and the marker commemorates their feat. Yet history failed
to record whether Aaron Wilson ever delivered the promised rum,
if only to drown the shame and horror of their folly.

The Galloping Spread
of Horse Theft

Convict #199, alias Davis Stephens, entered the State Prison at Windsor on August 2, 1816. There he was to spend ten years for horse theft. However, he found the jail so unappealing that he escaped on October 10. Recaptured the same day, Davis Stephens then became prisoner #211. For during his two-month stay, six other horse thieves had been corralled in that granite pen.

Theirs was such a specialized crime that the state prison's register differentiated between immates guilty of horse theft and those jailed for unspecified theft. The prison register also recorded the admission of the occasional roundup of partners and entire gangs, such as the December 31, 1830, jailing of horse thieves #726, #727, #728, and #729. Two of them got a ten-year term, one received seven years, and the fourth, a three-year sentence. The average sentence was for six years.

The number of horse thefts, of course, far exceeded the number of indictments, whereas the number of convictions was much less than the number of indictments. Many of the accused escaped conviction through the loopholes of legal technicalities; or because plaintiffs, prompted by the threat of house or barn-burning (a common occurrence), suddenly would withdraw the charges; or through corrupt law officers, lawyers, and judges.

To appreciate the seriousness of the crime, one should remem-

ber the importance of the horse before its replacement by the
combustion engine. The reins of a man's horse were indeed the
lifeline not only to his transportation but often to his livelihood.
Horse theft was a felony. When law enforcement was lax because
of the constabulary's collusion by indifference or inefficiency, or
because of the court's bribery-induced leniency, vigilante groups
sprang up to administer "justice" with lynchings. The crime also
created such enterprises as The Sherbourne Horse Theft Society.

To make a career of horse theft, a man had to be resourceful,
wily, agile, and have great stamina. He not only had to know
horses but the market for them. He needed dependable, widespread
contacts both for fencing his merchandise and for concealment
and protection. He often was adept at changing a horse's markings
and coloring with dyes, clippers, paints, and chemicals such as
nitrate of silver. One method of imprinting a white star on a
horse's forehead was to apply a hot, baked potato to it. The
process was repeated until the bleach took effect. Experts were
said to be able to change a horse's identity in less than fifteen
minutes. It sometimes happened that an owner, discouraged by a
long and costly search for his stolen horse, was conned into buying his own disguised horse, thinking the low price for such a
good replacement was "a real steal."

Before the animal was camouflaged, however, it had to be
stolen. The horse thieves carried rope, blindfolds, twine, and pieces
of flannel or burlap with which to muffle the sound of hooves and
to obscure tracks. Thefts were thoroughly planned, and they con-
ducted their forays on moonless nights. If a barn or pasture was
protected by a watchdog, the thief managed to silence it with a
knife or poison.

Daytime was also prime time. Horse thieves had choice pickings
at county fairs, sulky races, and all sporting and other events that
drew crowds from a wide area. The carriage sheds of country
churches, especially during weddings and funerals, offered good
prospects, as did well-patronized hotels, inns, and taverns. Another popular ploy was to hire a horse and carriage from a well-
stocked livery stable. The nominal deposit was sometimes paid
with counterfeit money. The advantage of ample time to flee a
considerable distance gave the theft a maximum chance of success.

The more accomplished horse thieves worked in teams. One served as a spotter and lookout. He often created a diversion, like picking a fight to attract—and distract—a crowd while his accomplice effected the theft and getaway. There were also profitable by-products of the trade, as there was a ready market for used buggies, sleighs, and other horse-powered vehicles, for assorted tack, and especially for wolf, bear, and buffalo robes.

No better—or worse—models of horse thieves than the Loomis Gang could serve to reveal the modus operandi of these criminals. Although horse theft in Vermont was prevalent well before 1802, that was the year twenty-three-year-old George Washington Loomis, Sr., fled the state, riding through the Winooski Valley pursued by a posse because of his extensive activities as the Green Mountain State's most notorious horse thief. He had prospered by taking stolen horses to Danby, Connecticut, from Randolph, Vermont, and also to Whitehall, New York. His exile to a secluded enclave in upstate New York, some thirty miles from Utica, neither checked his greed nor thwarted his resourcefulness. For there he established headquarters for his widespread operations. There he sired the Loomis Gang, a dynasty of criminals that flourished during most of the nineteenth century. There were five sons: Wash Jr., Plumb, Denio, Grove, and William.

The Loomis Gang formed a syndicate to more efficiently operate and expand its dealership in stolen horses. It especially prospered during the Civil War years. Because of the Union Army's need for artillery and cavalry horses, rising prices caused a rampage of horse theft.

Orange County was the breeding center for Vermont's famous Blackhawk and Morgan horses. The latter is the only breed ever to have been named for a specific horse, Justin Morgan. Because his progeny were known for their power, speed, endurance, disposition, and adaptability, they were in great demand and provided a highly profitable market for horse thieves.

The Loomises had established a chain of raiding and collection areas from which relays were run to points where the horses were sold. As agents for the transportation and sale of others' thefts, they got a 75 percent commission. If a horse was stolen by an independent operator, it could be sold to the Loomises for $25.00.

If the horse then was resold without any difficulties, the Loomises would pay the thief a $15.00 bonus. This arrangement gave the Loomises a loyal group of suppliers. It also gave the horse thieves a guaranteed buyer for their stolen merchandise. Historian George W. Walter reported that "Grove Loomis knew where every stolen horse was located." For a $50.00 fee Grove Loomis would even help their owners locate them. Therefore "whether the horses were returned or sold, the Loomis Gang always profited by the transaction." Their operations spread throughout New York state into Vermont and the other New England states, into Canada and even Pennsylvania.

Although horse theft was their specialty, the Loomises also excelled in wholesale thievery (including bank robbery), arson, embezzlement, counterfeiting, and murder. George W. Walter, the historian of the Loomis Gang, said "Like all great criminal organizations they learned early that the best legal talent was required to help outwit the law, and that judges and juries could be bribed." As the Loomises were well protected by lawyers, law enforcement officers, and judges, their crimes flourished.

Another method of concealing horses, besides altering their appearance, was discovered by Constable James L. Filkins whose long career was almost exclusively spent in his relentless pursuit of the Loomis Gang. He reported that, after he had discovered a secluded meadow in their vast domain, "I spent hours in there, sitting, watching and listening while trying to locate stolen horses. The hay from that meadow was kept piled on a big haystack. One time I found horse manure . . . but there was no sign of horses about. Once I was rewarded by my patience. I heard a horse's whinny. That whinny seemed to come from that big haystack. On closer examination of the stack I discovered a door neatly covered with hay. Opening the door, I found myself looking into a small horse barn filled with horses." Other less prominent horse thieves also used hollowed-out hay stacks.

One day Grove Loomis was outsmarted by some amazing horse sense. Herbert Throop, a farmer's young son, was very proud of his horse's accomplishments. He had trained his pet to dance, kneel, roll over, and play dead. One night it disappeared. Herbert and his father, Erastus, went to the Loomis place to demand the animal's return. As Grove was denying that he had the animal or even knew of its whereabouts, the loud whickering of a horse in the nearby pasture caught young Herbert Throop's attention. He walked over to inspect it. Although the horse's coloring and markings were different, its build and gait were similar to those of Herbert's pet. The boy gave the horse a command. It obeyed. Grove watched, amazed, as the horse responded to his young owner's orders to kneel, dance, roll over, and play dead. Grove stubbornly claimed that he had bought the horse from outside the state. The lad's father took the horse from the pasture, and they headed home. Grove did not follow them.

In Vermont as elsewhere, especially in Loomis territory, every horse was at some time vulnerable to theft. Consider the wholesale seizure of a colt and three fine horses that belonged to Harrison J. Sweet, a partner in the Marcy Horse Theft Detectives. According to the local paper, "They were taken from his pasture on Friday night. . . . Twelve members of the Horse Theft Detectives fanned out in every direction for clues. Before dark on Monday they found the horses at the Loomis farm." If the Loomises were indicted, no conviction was ever recorded for "like modern-day gangsters, they were well protected by attorneys, judges, and law officers," according to George Walter.

If automobiles had not replaced horses, making car theft one of this century's most common crimes, a third generation of the Loomis Gang might still be flourishing. Then if the State Prison at Windsor were still a prison, it would be host to convict #211's successors who, as car thieves, are the scourge of our automobile age.

Escape?

Seventy-six years before Chester's sticky-fingered phantom had made his bizarre escape from Windsor's Vermont State Prison, a Joseph Burnham also allegedly gained freedom after his "corpse" had been released for burial.

The forty-four-year-old Woodstock farmer had been sentenced to serve ten years at hard labor and fined $1,000 for the rape of a Pomfret girl. That was in June, 1826. Believing that the sentence was unwarranted, his son George of New York City, plus some prominent Woodstock friends and fellow Masons, promptly sought a pardon for the popular Woodstock citizen.

The fact that a pardon, not a retrial, was sought, tacitly acknowledged the prisoner's guilt. While the verdict was uncontested, the sentence presumably deserved a review. However, on October 15, 1826, before the brief for a pardon had been considered, Joseph Burnham mysteriously died. It was scarcely four months after his imprisonment. Two days later his body—or a substitution—was released to his son George and then buried in Woodstock's Cushing Cemetery.

Requiescat in pace. But the body interred as Joseph Burnham was not to rest in peace. For only a few months later, a rumor spread like the winds of autumn that a resurrected Joseph Burnham was living in Manhattan. Certain ambiguities about his death gave credence to the rumor. What was the cause of death? Why was it not entered on the obligatory death certificate? If the cause had been in doubt, why was there no autopsy? Why had the death certificate disappeared—unless the cause of death had been falsified? Why had the body been placed, unattended, in an isolated corridor of the jail; then taken to the prison's hospital several hours later? Was the time sufficiently long enough for a substitution to have been made with a corpse stolen from a fresh grave, as rumored? (At about this time several grave robbings had been discovered. Such cadavers supplied regional medical schools, including Woodstock's.)

So persistent was speculation about Joseph Burnham's alleged escape and macabre "death" that the *Woodstock Observer* exploited the rumor in a series of lurid dispatches. The first appeared on September 29, 1829. The newspaper published an interview with Vermont legislator R. Makepeace Ransom of Woodstock. In an article titled "Equal and Exact Justice," Ransom asked such challenging questions as: "How came young Mr. Burnham . . . to hear (of his father's death) and get to Windsor so soon? . . . Did not the nearest relatives of Joseph Burnham have a time revelling . . . on the night after the supposed corpse of Burnham was put in the tomb?"

Advocates of the rumor supported their belief with speculation that Joseph Burnham had arranged his "death" by having feigned attacks from an increasing onslaught of life-threatening mental and physical ailments. Then it was claimed that on Sunday, April 15, an accomplice (his son George?) had slipped him a drug which induced a coma that simulated death, but with the certainty or at least the expectation that once beyond the prison wall it would wear off.

Proponents of the escape theory further claimed that the corpse brought to the prison hospital that Sunday was not Joseph Burnham's, but a substitute; and that on Tuesday morning when George Burnham attended the burial, his not-so-late father was safely en route to New York City. He was said to have been seen there by Lyman Mower and Aaron Cutter, Woodstock acquaintances. Mower also claimed to have spoken with Joseph Burnham, according to their statements published in the October 13, 1829, issue of the *Woodstock Observer.*

One surmise spawned another. If Joseph Burnham had been spirited out of jail alive by a switch of bodies, there must have been accomplices. Burnham was said to have been a Mason. So, it was claimed, were the prison's physician, superintendent, and the prisoner's son George. Members of the fraternal order of the Free and Accepted Masons were secretive, militantly loyal to one another, and pledged to help any fellow Mason whose life, welfare, or liberty were in jeopardy. Suspicious outsiders, aroused by the Masons' secrecy and their mystical bond of loyalty to one another, generated hostility against them nationwide. (In Vermont the anti-Mason movement was so active that in the early 1830's its members elected a gubernatorial candidate.) Surely, they reasoned, Joseph Burnham's escape had been accomplished with the Masons' connivance. Yet contrary assertions held that such a conjecture was ridiculous, because, they insisted, Burnham was not a Mason.

The skeptics discounted Cutter's and Mower's claim that they had not only spoken to Joseph Burnham in New York City but that his alias was Patrick Dolon. For one thing, Mower himself, who had had minor skirmishes with the law, used the alias Joshua Cobb. He was, therefore, not a reliable witness. Neither was Cutter who also had an unsavory reputation; and the Patrick Dolon who was supposed to be Joseph Burnham, was not. Dolon merely resembled Burnham.

Because state prison officials were said to have been accomplices to Burnham's escape, the Vermont General Assembly appointed a commission to investigate the prisoner's death or escape. The commissioners were J. S. Pettibone and Robert Pierpoint. Meanwhile Woodstock's selectmen ordered the body in Burnham's grave exhumed. As it had been buried for three years, the examination failed to determine its identity. It was before the age of fingerprinting and dental records. A second disinterment also proved inconclusive. The state commission's examination of the prison records found nothing to confirm the allegation of fraud. It then pursued evidence of Mower's claim to have spoken to Burnham in New York City. An intermediary advised the commission that Mower would produce Burnham if a suitable reward was offered.

Mr. Pierpoint journeyed to Manhattan with the commission's

five hundred dollar reward plus the stipulation that Mower would only get it if Burnham returned to Vermont within fifteen days. Mr. Pierpoint knew that an escaped convict would not return willingly. So Mower was authorized to give Burnham the commission's promise of a full pardon if he cooperated. Commissioner Pierpoint also sent two of Burnham's former Woodstock acquaintances to New York to meet Dolon. Both denied that the man was Burnham. Therefore when a live Burnham failed to materialize, the escape theory collapsed.

On November 10, 1829, the *Woodstock Observer* and other Vermont newspapers published the commission's report. It stated that all available evidence indicated that Joseph Burnham indeed had died in the Windsor State Prison on October 15, 1826.

A good rumor dies hard. Despite the official close of the matter, conflicting facts and conjectures about Burnham's alleged tryst with freedom had—like Lizzie Borden's story—escaped the verdict of historical fact to become a legend. In 1832, six years after Burnham s death, his alleged escape was dramatized. The farce, in five acts, was titled *The Doleful Tragedy of the Raising of Jo. Burnham.* As late as 1882 the play had a successful tour of Vermont. *The Vermont Standard* reported this "most ridiculous of all stage performances . . . had a run never equaled in Vermont."

In August of 1975, the State Prison at Windsor closed. No longer would its ledger record the many escapes during its 166 years as the state's maximum security prison. Its brick-faced granite walls now enclose a residence for the elderly. Their enjoyment of the premises will never be disturbed by the ghosts of prisoners. For like many of those prisoners—including Joseph Burnham?—the ghosts have all escaped.

Grave Robbing, a Once Prevalent and Profitable Undertaking

What did French General Pétain and Mrs. Penfield Churchill have in common? Despite a world of differences, the similarity is unique.

General Pétain was both famous and infamous as a hero and traitor. His body was stolen for political reasons, whereas Mrs. Penfield Churchill was known only to God and the townspeople of Hubbardton, Vermont, until her obscurity ended one snowy November night when her grave was found empty. The discovery so enraged the townspeople that on November 29, 1830, some three hundred men marched five miles to Castleton Medical College. Only after having exacted a promise from the sheriff that no arrest would be made did the dean surrender the body to the crowd. "The Hubbardton Raid" was commemorated forty-nine years later by an oyster banquet attended by local and state dignitaries, including prominent doctors, who were entertained by a parody of Longfellow's *Hiawatha,* titled "Song of the Hubbardton Raid."

The episode is mentioned to show that throughout New England grave robbing or body snatching—or what doctors and their students more euphemistically called "resurrections"—was once a prevalent and profitable undertaking.

Bodies were needed by medical colleges for the teaching of

anatomy, for pathological research, and by physicians wanting to improve or perfect new surgical techniques. The only legal source of cadavers was through judges who, as an added penalty in sentencing murderers to death, directed that their corpses be given to a doctor for dissection. The disposal of a corpse for dissection therefore bore the stigma of ultimate disgrace.

After the growth of New England medical schools following the Revolutionary War, public outrage at the great increase in grave robbings prompted laws against it. No sooner had Dartmouth College opened its medical school in 1796 than New Hampshire's General Assembly enacted its first law against the practice. It provided a fine "not to exceed $1,000, imprisonment not to exceed one year, and public whipping not to exceed thirty-nine stripes." As Vermont's border is only a mile from Dartmouth, in 1804 its legislature passed a law with penalties similar to New Hampshire's. By 1820 all six New England states had statutes with comparable terms. The severity of punishment increased in direct proportion to the growth of medical schools and, with it, the increased number of medical students, according to Frederick C. Waite in his definitive study on the subject, titled "Grave Robbing in New England." He stated that while writing laws was merely one approach to the problem, the difficulty of enforcement was by far the greater problem. Most disinterments went undiscovered. Even if they were discovered, the culprits rarely were seized. Between 1820 and 1840 only seven indictments were recorded for the crime of grave robbing. During those twenty years there were more than 1600 medical students in Vermont's three medical colleges, located in Castleton, Burlington, and Woodstock.

Six students were usually assigned to one dissection. In a dissection with a preceptor (teacher), there often was only one corpse for the entire class. So at least four hundred cadavers were obtained to benefit all those students. The figure was determined, of course, by the availability of grave robbers and the diligence of their work. Nearly all the cadavers were illegally acquired, most of them from Vermont graveyards. In that twenty-year span, only one conviction for an illegal disinterment was recorded. The same condition prevailed throughout the other New England states, according to Dr. Waite. The enormity of the practice is apparent in the fact that some 15,000 New England medical students were graduated between 1801 and 1900. In addition were the uncounted dropouts and those whose medical education was achieved under preceptors, an apprenticeship system that was then a commonly accepted qualification for the practice of medicine. Thus, a few thousand is a reasonable estimate of the number of resurrections made during those years.

How did the mourners protect their dead from the voracious reapers? Of the three generally used methods the easiest was to fill the grave with sticks, large stones, or sheaves of straw, thus making digging harder and more time-consuming. Another method was to have a temporary interment in a public vault made of large granite or other stone blocks with securely locked iron doors. Such vaults still abound in New England cemeteries. Coffins were stored there for just long enough to let putrefaction render the cadavers undesirable for dissection, for this was before embalming was commonly practiced. The last method was to hire a grave watcher, who spent about ten evenings from dusk to dawn in the cemetery, accompanied by a shotgun. Yet there are records to show that this precaution was not always successful; for agents of the resurrectionists were known to ply these watchmen with liquor before they went on duty. So they either failed to assume their posts or were *hors de combat* at the grave. There were even records of the watchers having been bound and gagged. Some watchers fired on their attackers, but because birdshot was usually used, wounding was seldom fatal or even crippling. A report of one exception stated that the culprit's body was "awarded" to a local doctor for dissection.

Prime targets were cemeteries within twenty miles of the medical schools where bodies were in demand or on order, and graveyards sufficiently distant from in-town churchyards, dwellings, or well-travelled roads. Grave robbing was exclusively a night-shift enterprise.

With the spread of railroads after the Civil War, bodies were procured from greater distances, even from the South, where black corpses were available. According to Harvard's famous Dr. John Warren, that medical school's cadavers were obtained from

New York City agents. The bodies were pickled in brine; and barrels were labelled Beef, Pork, Hides, or Turpentine.

So skilled were body snatchers that discovery of their macabre loot was rare. Meticulous procedures, usually by an able-bodied, three-man team, were followed. First, they made their service known to medical school authorities, or to a preceptor, and thus established a liaison for orders. Second, they scouted a prospective burial. This sometimes required a tip-off agent or spotter, who sent a message, often in code, of time and place of burial.

Thirdly, they reconnoitered the locale, cemetery, and gravesite in daylight. This was accomplished by a stranger pretending to be a dog owner looking for his lost pet, or a hunter seeking small game, or a hobo merely passing through town.

Lastly, one man in charge of a wagon or carriage sought an inconspicuous place to park it later. The two others carefully noted the fresh grave, using a shaded lantern. This examination was important, for it was a common practice to have a friend or relative of the deceased decorate the grave with an intricate design with sticks, shells, stones, or flowers so that any disturbance could be detected. Thus it had to be precisely replaced. A light, called a dark lantern, was used because its beam could be well shaded. Many disinterments were thwarted by a poorly shaded lantern.

Two tarpaulins were indispensable. One was placed by the grave and piled with the excavated earth so that its return would leave no telltale residue on the grass. At the head of the grave an excavation of some three-feet square was dug until the coffin was located. Through the head of the coffin a line of holes was bored with an auger. A saw was unwieldy and an ax too noisy. The section was removed.

With a tool known as "the hook," the body was hauled from the coffin. The instrument was a five-foot-long iron bar with a hook shaped like a gaff pole. At the other end was a cross-bar handle. The hook was placed under the chin, and the corpse was pulled from the casket. The hook often badly damaged the jaw and the roof of the mouth. An alternative method was to use a harness, strapped beneath the arms, with a ring at the back through which a rope was fastened. (Perhaps the hook, and undue haste, accounted for the fact that the surrender of Mrs. Penfield

Churchill's body to the sheriff had to be made in two install-
ments.)

Usually the shroud or other clothing was removed and left in
the grave; for if such garments or personal effects were found,
they would make identification possible. The corpse then was
tightly wrapped and tied in the other tarpaulin.

The soil was shoveled back into the grave; the surface was
neatly restored; all implements were counted, then wrapped in
the first tarpaulin, which was tied carefully to prevent any tool
from being left behind to betray the robbers. The two bundles
were then toted to the carriage or wagon in only one trip by the
two muscular resurrectionists. The entire operation was said to
take one hour.

There are ample records of the apprehension of both body
snatchers and their customers. One, a doctor from Ipswich, Massachusetts, on whose premises were discovered identifiable parts
of three bodies, was defended by Daniel Webster. The good
doctor was fined $800. At Mr. Webster's suggestion he moved his
damaged practice to Washington, D. C., where he ultimately served
three of our presidents as their personal physician.

Yet the vast majority of grave robbings went undetected; a fact
that makes one wonder: How much of New England's preeminence
in the field of medical science is owed to the diligence—and success—of its grave robbers?

A Sampler
of Vermont Eccentrics

Eccentrics are as indigenous to Vermont as her fiddlehead ferns. That doesn't imply they are as "wild"; nor that their existence is as menacing to the foundations of Vermont society as are the termites which plague other New England states. Eccentricity has flourished throughout all of New England, for stubborn individualism is rooted in the character of its Yankees.

Yet Vermont's special climate of tolerance—some call it indifference—has long nurtured eccentrics. Perhaps this is because, as Ralph Nading Hill says in his book *Contrary Country: A Chronicle of Vermont,* "Vermont itself is an eccentric." He justified the allegation by stating that "before the federal government declared war on Germany in 1917, Vermont appropriated one million of her precious dollars for war purposes. . . . And in 1941, Vermont declared war on Japan before Washington did." To certify Vermont's eccentricity beyond a reasonable doubt, Mr. Hill concluded, "Since the Civil War, it has been the only state that has always been Republican."

Whoever would disparage eccentrics as "wild" has little appreciation for integrity and less respect for individuality. Nor could he understand eccentricity because he ignores the third factor in the making of an eccentric. That ingredient is obsession, the motive force behind every eccentric. The obsessions can be as different as a revelation of visions, greed, a love of statistics, the dread

of germs, the worship of math, a craving for immortality or anonymity, or simply the need to outrun a fox.

When it does not incite ridicule, eccentricity arouses awe or
even envy, for often it is an aberration of genius. Yes, genius. According to philosopher John Stuart Mill, "the amount of eccentricity in a society has been proportional to the amount of genius,
mental vigor, and moral courage it contained. That so few now
dare to be eccentric marks the chief danger of the time." Surely
it is as true today as it was in Mill's nineteenth century.

Four religious creeds were founded by Vermonters. The agony
and ecstasy of their visions and revelations, and the zealotry they
inspired, were met with ridicule and outright hostility. Its inten-
sity was proportional to the growth of their following.

One of these visionaries was John Humphrey Noyes. In 1848
Mr. Noyes founded a religious community at Putney, Vermont.
It was an experiment in communal living. The members, who were
later called "Bible communists," believed that only by commun-
ion with God, and the total sharing of all personal possessions
could they achieve perfection. The doctrine, known as *perfectionism,* included the sharing of wives and husbands—a practice
called *complex marriage.* This religious conviction was too complex for their monogamous neighbors who, through either moral
outrage or envy, caused them to move to Oneida, New York.
Thereafter the sect was known as the Oneida Community, and
there they prospered. The sect manufactured and sold steel game
traps, which a member had invented. Factories sprang up that
also made a variety of chains and canning supplies. Great prosperity confirmed their belief that all work was dignified. They
also believed that women had equal rights with men, a notion
that some people still regard as eccentric.

In the suffering and death at the Battle of Bennington, atheist
William Miller found religion—his own. It sprang from an obsession
with death and Judgment Day. This self-appointed prophet of
doomsday predicted that the world would end on October 22,
1844. Consequently some half a million Millerites were seized
with hysteria. One was a Chester, Vermont, farmer. He had a
seamstress make "ascension robes" for six of his choicest cows.
Because on the fateful day that Prophet Miller had said would be

the world's last, the Chester farmer claimed "they'll come in mighty handy up there. It's a long trip, and the kids will be wanting some milk."

Another free-thinker was Ethan Allen. That flamboyant land-speculator, soldier-hero, politician, and self-proclaimed philosopher was also an atheist turned deist. He wrote an ineloquent diatribe against the influential Congregational Church titled *Oracles of Reason.* Fortunately for Vermont's history, Ethan Allen's sword was not as blunt as his pen.

Yes, free-thinking was a characteristic Vermont indulgence. Another practitioner was named Dorril. He was a deserter from General Burgoyne's army who founded a cult of vegetarianism. The Dorrilites were such strict vegetarians that not only would they not eat God's manna of creatures, neither would they be shod, dressed, or gloved in animal skins. Preacher Dorril had declared that no arm could ever be raised against him. The sect disintegrated shortly after he was knocked to the floor in church by a free-thinking, free-swinging non-believer.

Vermont's most famous visionary was Joseph Smith of Sharon. In 1830 he founded the Church of Jesus Christ of Latter-day Saints, whose members are known as Mormons. When he was only eleven, Joseph Smith experienced the first of his visions which, some years later, led to his announced discovery of gold plates that "told the history of the true church of Christ." The church's *Book of Mormon* is said to be the transcription of these plates. His visions continued throughout his ministry. He ruled the church community by the magnetic delivery of his "revelations" which attracted an enormous following. Prophet Smith's power and political ambitions—he declared he would be a candidate for president—and his advocacy of polygamy made him unpopular among the "gentiles," as the Mormons called non-believers. Smith and some followers destroyed a hostile newspaper, and its editor fled. The thirty-nine-year-old zealot was jailed. A mob broke in and killed him. He was succeeded by Brigham Young, a fellow Vermonter from Whitingham. Pastor Young is mentioned here not because of his long and successful church leadership, but because he practiced what he preached, which was the "divine" sanction of polygamy. He had at least seventeen wives. When he died at seventy-six, he left fifty-six children. Any man who assumed the expense and management of that many wives and children amply qualifies as an eccentric.

Brattleboro's James Fisk was an apostle of greed. That was his obsession. He also indulged other insatiable appetites. His robust humor incited an onslaught of pranks that generated both mirth and ire, and which only subsided when in his teens he joined a circus. Thereafter his flamboyance became a circus in itself. He dressed like a ringmaster. His girth expanded with his ego. Soon Jim returned to Brattleboro. To compete with his peddler-father, he bought a wagon, painted it in the festive, gaudy colors of a circus wagon, and with four spirited horses set out to make his fortune. It did not take long. For he spun yarns as well as sold yard goods, and he was efficient, hard-working, and shrewd yet honest. In less than two years he operated five multicolored wagons, but always restless, he sold out in 1860 and joined Boston's Jordan Marsh & Company. When war was declared, he invaded Washington to make Jordan's the outfitter-supplier of the Union army. He was so successful that not only did Jordan's have to expand, they made Jim a partner. After the war the scent of money led him to Wall Street. He became a gluttonous speculator.

Soon tycoon Fisk had joined forces with Jay Gould and other speculators. He became a director of the Erie Railroad, and by illegal manipulations outsmarted Cornelius Vanderbilt to seize control of the company. No longer a paragon of Yankee thrift and virtue, he bought New York's Grand Opera House where he and Gould produced extravaganzas. With his purchase of the Narragansett Steamship Line, he donned a musical comedy-version of an admiral's uniform. He and Gould nearly cornered the gold market. Greed, in the enticement of lust, proved his undoing. Josephine Mansfield, his shrewd, luxury-loving mistress, was also having an affair with Jim's good friend, Edward S. Stokes. The two tried to blackmail Jim. Jim had them both charged with blackmail. They brought countersuits. Stokes, who saw his lawsuit become hopeless and himself exposed as a blackmailer, shot and killed Jim Fisk, aged thirty-seven. After a gaudy funeral it was discovered that Fisk had been secretly supporting many poor people. It was indeed ironic that the greedy Brattleboro rapscallion's only altruistic deed was the indulgence—and extent—of his philanthropy.

Nowadays computers are commonplace. In 1810 they were unheard of, except for a six-year-old Cabot, Vermont, genius named Zerah Colburn. He was locally famous at that age for his feats of mathematical calculations. His fame spread as the problems grew so lengthy and complex that his skeptical inquisitors—all expert mathematicians—took longer and longer to confirm his almost instantaneous answers. He appeared at Dartmouth and Harvard to confound their experts. To the challenge of "how many seconds in 2000 years?" young Zerah thought a moment, and unhesitatingly replied, "730,000 days, 17,520,000 hours, 1,051,200,000 minutes, 63,072,000,000 seconds." He was right. Inevitably he was exploited. After a tour of important American cities he went to Europe. Napoleon gave him a scholarship to the Lyceum Napoleon. England's Earl of Bristol gave Zerah a scholarship to Westminster School, which he attended for four years. His father, who had accompanied him to Europe, died there of tuberculosis. Fifteen years after he had left Cabot, Zerah returned, penniless. His old mother scarcely recognized him, nor did his six brothers and two sisters. After failing at teaching, he joined Burlington's Congregational church; then became a Methodist preacher. He left the ministry to better support his wife and three daughters, and spent the last five years of his life as a professor of languages at Norwich University. Despite Zerah's genius, the equation of how to achieve a normal life eluded him.

Another genius of Zerah Colburn's stamp was a man from Barnet, Vermont, named McCulloch. He was "a living almanac." He could tell the day, month, and year of an event. His total recall could produce such minutiae as "whom he had heard preach on a given date, the text, the psalm and the tune to which the psalm was sung." History does not record how Mr. McCulloch's capacity for and obsession with trivia shaped his destiny.

West Windsor's Daniel Leavens Cady longed for immortality. Through hard work and considerable intelligence, this pear-shaped, pompous pedant and egomaniac had achieved most of his earthly goals. He had put himself through college; married a suitably cultured and conveniently wealthy Burlington woman; became a lawyer and prominent judge; and distinguished himself as a widely read columnist and poet. In addition to himself, he loved literature, liquor, and travel. His taste in mausoleums was apparently influenced by Napoleon's tomb, for his own was similarly designed. Two bronze tablets, one on the inside, bore a lengthy epitaph he had composed in Latin. If he could not take his wealth with him, neither would he share eternity with his wife, so the enormous mausoleum was designed for his sole occupancy. Despite the employment its construction provided West Windsorites, Mr. Cady was not loved by his hometown. It was not solely because of his pretentiousness or tippling. It was more likely because his tomb occupied prime pasture land, and because its exorbitant cost could—like manure—have done more good if it had been spread elsewhere.

Willingly or not, eccentrics often are loners because of their unconventional ways. Near the little town of Kirby lived Russell Risley, a loner with a difference. He peopled his life—and his barn—with neighbors and prominent figures whom he portrayed with house paint. So lifelike were his subjects that the curious traveled many miles to see them. One section of barn siding featured a shapely nude woman. Was she a fantasy of bachelor Risley's, or a rendition of a real person? The townspeople's speculation was never answered. He also populated his pasture with busts of recognizable citizens, and animals hewn from logs and pasture granite. Every available space in his house had paintings of people, animals, and landscapes. Despite the fame such talent brought, he was indeed a loner, preferring his renditions to the models. So at his gate he posted the sign Smallpox. His genius also extended to other fields. He invented a wired trapeze on which to swing from house to barn. It had a satellite to transport his milk pails. He was said to be the first to pipe sap into his sugarhouse, and in old age he taught himself French well enough to enjoy a weekly French newspaper.

Some people live bizarre lives to escape being themselves. Such an eccentric was the mysterious "Captain Thunderbolt," later Dr. John Wilson. He appeared in Dummerston, Vermont, in 1818, from England; he was well educated, tall, suave, and charming. Why then had he picked Dummerston when he could have a successful practice in London, Boston, or any large city? His dignity and reserve protected him from inquisitive townspeople so his background remained a mystery, which added to his appeal. He was an excellent doctor who supplemented the income from so limited a practice by teaching school. He had, however, a number of quirks. Never would he open his door until he knew who the caller was. Winter and summer he wore a silk scarf, which was not then fashionable, yet he was otherwise elegantly attired. At dances he was oddly unstable despite his fine bearing, and the contra dances' twists and turns would spill him to the floor.

In 1823 he moved to Newfane. Although the townspeople there knew he was a hard drinker, it never curtailed his availability or skill. In 1835 he moved to Brattleboro. Women found him magnetically attractive even after he had married a Brattleboro woman. They had a son whom he raised with admirable devotion after his wife's early death. One day in his late sixties he summoned a doctor and another friend to his deathbed. He was fully clothed, even to his scarf and shoes. He tried to exact a promise that he was to be buried fully dressed, scarf, shoes and all. However an undertaker undressed him to wash and embalm the body. The scarf had concealed a large red scar. His left leg, which was withered as if from a childhood paralysis, had an old bullet wound and part of the heel had been shot off. A thick cork wedge had replaced it. Only Dr. Wilson's extraordinary will power had concealed his lameness, for he never had betrayed a limp. But why? Surely he had something to conceal. Indeed he did!

From old records of wanted men, the sheriff discovered that the neck scar, withered leg, and cork heel belonged to a notorious British highwayman called Captain Thunderbolt because of the speed and cunning of his forays. He liked the name. While holding up a coach, he exercised great courtesy. He robbed only the men, kissed the women, and announced that they had just been inconvenienced by Captain Thunderbolt. He was born John Doherty, in Scotland. Sometimes he dressed as a priest, and could discourse on religion like a theologian. Once he had fled to northern Ireland where he first practiced medicine. Later he fled to America with a young accomplice named Michael Martin, nicknamed Captain Lightfoot. Then they lost touch with one another, perhaps intentionally. It was Michael Martin who told his Cambridge, Massachusetts, jailers about John Doherty, alias Captain Thunderbolt, alias Dr. John Wilson, before he, Captain Lightfoot, was hanged in 1821 for a Dedham, Massachusetts, robbery. Having survived his careers as highwayman, teacher, doctor, and bon vivant, "Dr. Wilson" died in bed—with his boots on—in May of 1847.

A benign touch of insanity is as sure a way to eccentricity as genius. Folks in Calais, Vermont, claim that Pardon Jones, who had once represented them ably in the state legislature, "went haywire." The evidence confirms it. He had developed a phobia about germs. So great was his fear of contamination that he had strapped a short pitchfork to his wrist to avoid touching his fellow men, and women, too. Store clerks took payment from a little tin pail hung from the fork, and deposited the change in it. His record in the legislature—when he was normal—never obtained for him the immortality of fame that he had achieved when he was not.

Andrew Blair, of Goshen Gore, proved that one can join the ranks of famous eccentrics with only one deed—in one giant step. Andrew agreed that fox hunting is good exercise for both the pursuer and prey. Yet the fox has more at stake. Andrew considered this unsportsmanly. He would make it a fair contest. So the next time he spotted a fox, he chased it—on foot—and captured it. Andrew suspected that the fox's initial surprise had denied the critter a good start, which he thought was an unfair advantage. So he told the fox that they would have another go at it. Go they did, after Andrew gave the fox "a few rods start." Through thickets, over hills and fences they ran. Again he was the victor, and Andrew Blair is remembered as the Vermonter who outran and thus outfoxed a fox.

Vermont's of Health and Wealth

Long before autumn's foliage and winter's ski slopes became the wellsprings of Vermont's tourist industry, her mineral springs brought forth a geyser of economic growth that considerably enriched the state's development. Vermont's health industry flourished from 1781 to the 1930's.

Mineral springs abounded throughout the length and breadth of the state—in eleven of the fourteen counties. According to Hemenway's *Vermont Historical Gazetteer* of 1868, over twenty spas catered to their patrons' appetites for panaceas, recreation, and the social whirl. People came from the Eastern Seaboard states, Canada, and the Midwest. Before the Civil War the springs were a popular tonic for Southerners, many of whom brought their slave servants. Thereafter, however, their desertion of abolitionist Vermont amounted to a boycott.

Far more numerous than the spas were the many claims of the water's curative effects, heralded by the extravagant claims of their promoters. One of the largest spas was the Missisquoi Springs at Sheldon. Each of its four sources had a different chemical complex. The Missisquoi's Broadway, New York, promotional office issued a brochure in 1868 claiming: "The curative properties of the Missisquoi Spring, which for many years were locally known, have now a widespread reputation and are fully established. Hundreds, if not thousands, have drank of its waters, and all concur in ascribing to them wonderful efficacy, and bear witness to the marvelous cures produced by their use. The Water of the Missisquoi Spring has cured: Cancer, Tumors of the Ovaria, Scrofula, Eczema, Catarrh, Bright's Disease of The Kidneys, Diabetes, Rheumatism, Dropsy, Salt-Rheum, Syphilis, Mercurial Sores, Constipation, Weak and Diseased Eyes, Piles, Dyspepsia, all Cutaneous Affections, and many ills that flesh is heir to." It bore testimonials by such prominent citizens as C. K. Garrison (the famous New York lawyer), Vermont's ex-governor John Gregory Smith, and Cyrus H. McCormick, the inventor of the reaper.

The history of the Missisquoi Spring is somewhat typical of the discovery, development, and exploitation of Vermont's mineral waters. Its spring-to-riches saga began in 1865 when wealthy New York lawyer, C. Bainbridge Smith "was cured of cancer of the tongue by the mineral waters of Sheldon." He had stopped to visit Governor John Gregory Smith, a relative, when en route to Canada. He had a life expectancy of only several months. Mrs. Smith urged him to try a bottle of the water from "the old Kimball spring." He did, and felt so much better, so soon, that after six weeks' treatment, he resumed his law practice. It was said that the spring's healing qualities had been known for nearly a century. So pleased with the spring's curative effects was its owner, Moses Kimball, that he made it free to all comers. However, Lawyer Smith, who also was an astute businessman, paid $500 for Kimball's spring plus $24,000 for its farm site. After having had the water analyzed, he bottled it under its new name, The Missisquoi Springs. By 1868 the springs produced "14,792 boxes, each holding twenty-four quart bottles of the precious fluid" for shipment throughout this country, Canada, and Europe, according to historian Louise Koier.

In Sheldon alone, three other springs became flourishing spas: the Sheldon, the Central, and the Vermont. Within a few years the flow of some three thousand summer folks supported not only its ten hotels and guest houses but a grocery, two new stores, a well-stocked livery stable, and a private hospital. The bonanza ended abruptly in 1870. For the giant Missisquoi Springs Hotel was destroyed by a fire, allegedly set by a psychotic cook. The hotel (which had been host to celebrities like Henry Ward Beecher and Edwin Stanton, Lincoln's Secretary of War) had been the social nucleus of Sheldon's health industry. Its orchestra played for balls, provided dinner music, and gave free concerts. With the end to the bottling of Missisquoi water, many of the community's summer guests departed. The geyser of profits had ceased.

Among the benefits attributed to the Middletown Mineral Springs in Rutland County were the cure of rickets, scurvy, ulcers, and impotence. One testimonial to the water's curative treatment for impotence should have been the astonishing fecundity recorded by Rutland's Edna Faith Connell who stated (in the November 1, 1939, issue of *The Vermonter)* that "In 1797 there were eight families living there, having a total of 113 children. . . . Not one of the eight men ever had but one wife, and there was only one pair of twins in the lot, and only sixteen years difference between the first born of all the families."

Middletown's springs were on the grounds of the great Hotel Montvert, which could accommodate 350 guests. The springs were said "to have been used by white men until 1811 and, according to tradition, for an untold prior period by the aborigines." Its famous waters were bottled and sold by grocery stores and drugstores. According to Louise Koier in her 1957 *Vermont Life* article "These Wonderful Waters," Middletown springs disappeared in 1811 in the aftermath of a flood that obliterated them with layers of gravel and silt. Yet fifty-seven years later, in 1868, the springs miraculously reappeared. For the compacted debris had been swept away by a heavy June flood, revealing additional springs (for a total of five), all of which had different chemical properties. The waters were soon bottled. Two years later a five-story hotel opened for the swarm of health-seekers. Despite claims of incredible cures that had spread throughout the East, one skeptic scoffed, saying "[The water] will not raise the dead or cure incurable diseases." The hotel was razed in 1906.

To remain unheralded—but not unnamed—were these other spas: Mt. Holly's Green Mountain Mineral Spring, Brookline's Spring, Windham's Vermont Mineral Springs, St. Albans's Wilden Spring, Lunenburg's Chalybeate Spring, Barre Mineral Springs, and Sudbury's Sulphur Springs.

The persistence of legend often passes for the authenticity of
historical fact. The origin of Vermont's first spa is illuminated by
just such conjecture. It presumably began in 1776 when Asa
Smith, a mystic from Clarendon, had a dream that a miraculous
spring in town would heal his "scrofulous humor." So vivid was his
vision that he not only claimed that he "saw" the exact spot but
its chemical identity was revealed to him as "chalybeate water
impregnated with lime." Despite his painfully crippling affliction,
Asa Smith penetrated the wild terrain, drank the water, poulticed
his inflamed joints with mud, and on returning to town and cabin
was allegedly cured. He was not alone. Other contemporary Vermonters had discovered the power of local waters. Following
deer trails, earlier settlers in Brunswick, Tunbridge, and South Hero
had found mineral waters rich in sulphate of magnesia, sulphur-
ated hydrogen gas, sulphate of potassium and soda, iodine of
magnesium, and peroxide of iron. It was said that local farmers
had to avoid many freshets "because they were so impregnated
with epsom salts as to be unfit for family use." The 1782 discovery of Newbury's mineral springs preceded the others. However, George Rounds, a shrewd neighbor of Clarendon's Asa
Smith, is credited with having established Vermont's first real spa.
In 1781 he had constructed a boarding-house cabin, with bath,
adjacent to Smith's spring. Its success resulted in his erecting a
frame hotel in 1798. Its second reconstruction became the
famous, elegant, three-storied Clarendon House. It had a capacity
of 250 guests, and a seasonal total of 2500 health and pleasure
seekers.

Clarendon House's season was from May 15 to the end of October. Its rates were: "Board per week-$10.00 to $12.00, Children
under 12 yrs. going to first table-$6.00; Servants-$6.00; Board
per day-$2.50. Amusements: billiards, bowling alley, croquet,
hiking, swimming, fishing, etc. Livery: A good livery connected
with the Hotel, plus accommodations for private carriages." The
brochure also stated that "While the invalid is restored to health,
through the agency of the medicinal properties contained in the
water, the businessman's mind [is] rendered elastic by having removed from it an undue weight of care and anxiety."

Scarcely two years after Clarendon House opened, William Wallace converted his tavern, near Newbury's sulphur springs, into the Spring Hotel. Locally it was known as "the house on the river road." It was soon to be more widely known as The Montebello Mineral Springs when it catered to invalids from Massachusetts, New Hampshire, Maine, and New York.

A well-worn trail of animal tracks was said to have revealed Tunbridge's mineral springs. That was in 1805. Yet the 1850's were the era of the greatest statewide growth of health resorts. Among them were two at Alburg Springs, those at Hardwick, Highgate, Plainfield, Vergennes' Elgin Spring, Williamstown, and Brunswick, where a fountain dispensed waters from six springs, each with its own mineral complexity. Besides iron, calcium, magnesium, white sulphur and bromide, one also had arsenic. Woodstock's Dearborn Spring was a latecomer. Actually it was the rediscovered Sanderson's mineral spring that had flourished in the early 1800's. The setting was magnificent. Its imposing hotel, built in 1890, was the hub of a terraced fifteen-acre park with carriage drives that led to the spring.

An emphasis on tennis, golf, boating, fishing, and scenic drives accounted for the long life of South Hero's Iodine Spring House. Its spa, however, remained a strong magnet. Manchester's Equinox House was one of Vermont's most glamorous spas. Its Equinox Ginger Champagne and Equinox Water were bottled there and marketed nationwide. On August 23, 1864, its guest register showed that rooms #51, #50, and #27 were assigned to Mrs. Abraham Lincoln, son Tad, and a servant. Robert Lincoln, another son, arrived a day later. It was the first lady's second visit.

Brattleboro's Wesselhoeft Water Cure was the state's strangest and most enduring spa, as well as a cultural phenomenon. It thrived from 1845 to about 1872. It was patronized by such celebrities as poets Lowell and Longfellow, Julia Ward Howe, William Dean Howells, Elisha Kune (the Arctic explorer), Civil War generals Sherman and McClellan, Helen Hunt Jackson, and ex-president Martin Van Buren. It was founded by a German political refugee, Dr. Robert Wesselhoeft, who had arrived in America in 1840. The next year the University of Pennsylvania awarded him an M.D. degree. His specialty was hydrotherapeutics, and a grateful Brattleboro patient, Mrs. Lovell Farr, encouraged him to settle in town, perhaps with the lure of financing him. His satisfaction with the site was voiced in a letter to the journalist Horace Greeley. "The water," he wrote, "is the purest I could find among several hundred springs from Virginia to the White Mountains." His Brattleboro Hydropathic Institution opened in May, 1845. It was a no-nonsense treatment center. The furnishings were simple, the food plain, the "cure" rugged. The treatment began at 4:00 A.M. when the patient was swaddled in thick blankets and "stewed in his own juices until his coverings were soaked." Then, unwrapped, he was quickly immersed in a bedside tub of cold water. There he stayed with the windows open "until a thick scum formed on the water. This wholesome exchange of matter" presumably purified the patient's system. Once dressed, the patient went outdoors for a walk, and imbibed the mineral waters. Only then could he have a breakfast of mush and milk, and bread and butter. So popular was this water cure that the next year when the patronage reached almost four hundred, local boarding houses took the overflow. Board and room plus baths and treatment cost $10 per day. Dr. Wesselhoeft died in 1852. (A former staff member then left the establishment to found "The Lawrence Water Cure." Despite the handsome, well-appointed premises, it lasted less than four years.)

Dr. Wesselhoeft's legacy proved to be cultural uplift rather than remedial health, for a group of his friends, fellow German emigrés, were fine musicians. (The most famous was organist Christian Schuster.) These artists formed the nucleus of Brattleboro's six musical groups: the Cornet Band, the Brattleborough Drum Corps, the Cotillion Band, the Brattleborough Musical Society, the Brattleborough Brass Band, and the Brattleborough Quadrille Band. This cultural renaissance spurred a number of prominent Americans to settle there. Their business acumen and community patronage enriched Brattleboro's industry, culture, and social life.

The gradual decline of Vermont's health industry was caused by the retreat of southern patronage after the Civil War, by fire, the Great Depression, and inevitably the miracle of immunization and therapies that poured from the wellsprings of our universities and pharmaceutical laboratories. Surely another subtle yet pervasive factor was the changing recreational, social, and economic patterns of American family life. Yet the long era of Vermont's mineral springs was an economic panacea for many communities, just as Vermont's scenery must have been a tonic to its health seekers.

The Underground Railroad Via Vermont

Just as the Holy Roman Empire was neither holy, Roman, nor an empire, so the Underground Railroad was neither subterranean nor a railroad. For transportation was more often by foot or wagons loaded with man-sized crates and barrels, some labelled "turpentine," "pork," "hides," etc. There were wagons with false bottoms so that when seemingly empty they could relay their human freight north. There was also ferry service. Steamboats on South Bay and Lake Champlain secreted "cargo" destined for St. John's Canada. (St. Albans's most prominent Underground agent, Hon. Lawrence Brainerd, who was not only the developer and director of the Vermont and Canada Railroad but an investor in steamboat construction and operations on Lake Champlain, used his authority and facilities to expedite the shipment of fugitives to Canada.) Yet no more graphic metaphor than *Underground Railroad* could describe the network of "stations" in over sixty Vermont communities through which countless runaway slaves fled to freedom via Vermont.

The fugitives were countless because the illegal traffic was secret. For under the federal constitution's Fugitive Slave Law of 1793, "state magistrates must aid in the arrest of fugitives. . . . They must certify them back to slavery and permit the masters or their agents to remove them from the state." The amount of traffic is evident in the fact that two Norwich Underground "conductors" alone, Stephen Boardman and Deacon Sylvester Morris, aided some six hundred slaves; and Norwich was not even on the main line. Vermont's defiance of the 1850 Fugitive Slave Law was evident in the annual increase of escapes to Canada of about two thousand runaways. Secrecy was also imperative to thwart Vermont's slave hunters whose diligence was incited by large rewards for captured fugitives. Often the slave owners or their agents joined the pursuits. The following incidents illustrate the conflict between the pursuers and the runaways' abolitionist protectors.

In 1812 a New York slave owner named Glen tried to repossess his slave from the man's Vermont protector, a Mr. Hodge, and the slave was legally returned in compliance with the Fugitive Slave Law of 1793. Three years later, however, Middlebury's Judge Theophilus Harrington refused to allow a runaway's return to slavery despite proof of ownership. He forbade the man's extradition claiming that the only proof of ownership he would honor was "a bill of sale from God Almighty." Judge Harrington's stand instituted a tradition of noncompliance in the courts. His moral precedent was justified by Vermont's constitution which in 1777 was the first constitution to prohibit slavery. It was not until fourteen years later (in 1791) that the independent republic of Vermont joined the new nation.

Occasionally townspeople spontaneously rescued slaves from the clutches of owners or their agents. In 1820 the great abolitionist, Horace Greeley, witnessed such a rescue in Poultney, which he described in his *Recollections of a Busy Life.*

So busy was Burlington's chief Underground operator, Lucius H. Bigelow, that his house was under constant surveillance by southern manhunters and local "bounty hunters." Yet one night he and his accomplices, the Reverend Joshua Young and Salmon Wires, who had been routed out of their beds, spirited six fugitives to St. Albans where they were put aboard a Central Vermont train to Montreal. Three of the runaways were the coachman, houseboy, and butler from the same Virginia plantation.

Another incident involving Mr. Bigelow concerned a runaway who had stayed in Burlington long enough to have bought a house.

His children were born there. He was a waiter in a hotel near the station when one day he saw his master in the dining room, and confided his plight to Mr. Bigelow. That very afternoon the man was on the train to Canada, his fare paid by his benefactor. Mr. Bigelow explained the hasty disappearance to the man's wife, then she and her children joined him. After he had sold their house and possessions, Mr. Bigelow sent them the proceeds.

Municipal records and diaries show that numbers of blacks were sidetracked, voluntarily settling in Vermont communities. Some had been able to buy their freedom. Others had not. Burlington's Tony Anthony was a conductor on the Underground Railroad, as were Hartland's Taylor Groce and Solomon Northrop. During the Civil War, West Windsor's Thomas Little and Abel Prince travelled to Boston to enlist in the Union Army's all-black 54th Massachusetts Regiment led by a Boston blue blood, Col. Robert Gould Shaw.

Ever since its constitutional prohibition of slavery in 1777, Vermont's abolitionist fervor was widespread and unrelenting. William Lloyd Garrison, the antislavery editor of *The Liberator,* said "Abolitionism was indigenous to the soil of Vermont." The antislavery movement was strong because on pragmatic grounds Vermont had no economic dependence on slave labor. Unlike other New England states, there was no agricultural, commercial/ maritime, or social intercourse with the South. Whereas on moral grounds, Vermonters' traditional commitment to freedom was a principle exemplified by their participation in the Civil War. Per capita, more Vermonters served than any other Northerners, one in every four adult males. Of those, fewer than 10 percent were drafted.

From 1833 numerous antislavery societies sprang up throughout the state. The first of these was in Jamaica. A year later the Vermont Anti-Slavery Society was founded, and by 1837 there were eighty-nine member towns. Where there were antislavery societies, there often were Underground Railroad stations. The first was founded by Quakers. In time, citizens from all facets of their separate communities and counties had united to create a vast Underground Railroad system.

The two main routes ran roughly north and south, with numer-

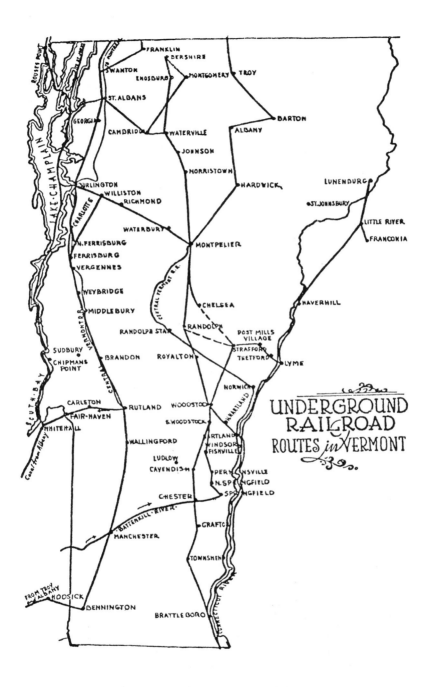

From Vermont's Anti-slavery and Underground Railroad Record, *by William Henry Siebert (New York: Negro University Press, 1969).*

ous "trunk lines" intersecting them. A roster of those townspeople who engineered and operated the network of silent whistle-stops to freedom included clergymen, lawyers and judges, journalists, doctors, innkeepers, farmers, teachers, tradesmen, plus municipal and state officials, including some Vermont governors.

The Underground Railroad's western flank ran from Bennington to Burlington, and on to St. Albans, Swanton, and Franklin. Way stops were Manchester, Wallingford, Rutland, Brandon, Middlebury, Weybridge, Vergennes, Ferrisburg, and Georgia. Bennington's chief Underground Railroad operator was Dr. Samuel Wilcox. Burlington's operators were better known than those of other communities. In addition to Messrs. Bigelow, Young, Wires, and ex-slave Anthony were Professor Dean, George Benedict, Samuel Huntington, and the Reverend John Converse who was the secretary of the Vermont Colonization Society, a movement to provide a homeland for ex-slaves. Brandon's Robert V. Marsh and editor Adrian T. Ramsey relayed fugitives to Ferrisburg's Quaker Roland T. Robinson who expedited their journey to Georgia, seventeen miles beyond Burlington. There the Reverend Alvah Sabin continued the slaves' travels to St. Albans.

The eastern flank ran from Brattleboro to Montpelier, from which three branches spread north. One "switching station" was along the Battenkill River valley. There the Underground depots were revealed by a row of chimney bricks painted white. Springfield, its eastern depot, was operated by a Dr. Crain and the inventor Noah Safford. Another branch's station progressions were Cambridge to Montgomery, Berkshire, Waterville, Enosburg, St. Johnsbury, Hardwick, Albany, Barton, and Troy. The stations along this main stretch of the eastern Underground Railroad and their abolitionist-operators were: Brattleboro's Willard Frost, Townshend's W. R. and Oscar Shafter, Grafton's John Barrett, Hartland's Methodist minister John Smith, Chester's Ocamel Hutchinson and Asa Davis, and Cavendish's Ryland Fletcher, later to be governor of Vermont. Included were South Woodstock's Col. Thomas Powers and Daniel Runsom along with his two sons Daniel, Jr., and Richard. Colonel Powers and Mr. Runsom owned the Kedron Tavern (now the Kedron Valley Inn) where in the cellar they hid their fugitive guests. The Underground Railroaders also listed Woodstock's Hon. Titus Hutchinson, Perkinsville's Judge Pingree, and Felchville's Mr. Bowen. The line encompassed West Windsor, Windsor, Hartland Four Corners, Norwich, and Lunenburg. Windsor's Underground shelter was said to have been under the roof of Judge Stephen Jacob's house, the same Judge Jacob who himself kept a slave, Dinah, for seventeen years. In this instance, expediency took precedence over principle (as it did with Thomas Jefferson who philosophically opposed slavery yet made no provision in his will to free his two hundred slaves). Then on to Strafford's operators, Deacon and Mrs. Morris; thence to Thetford and to Post Mills Village's Lyman Hinckley, a Baptist deacon, and to Chelsea's Wilder Deerborn.

The eastern route's conductors also included Randolph's Howard Griswold, and Montpelier's Col. Jonathan Peckham Miller and newspaper editor Joseph Poland, who knew more of the operators of both main lines than anyone. Colonel Miller gave much time and money to the abolitionist cause. In 1840 he and another Vermonter went to London to represent their state at the World's Anti-Slavery Convention. From the 1840's to 1850's the Underground Railroad had its greatest volume of traffic.

The progression of stations and their diligent operators continued with Waterbury's Dr. Arms along with Deacons Butler and Parker, to Richmond's William P. Briggs and E. A. Stanbury, to Williston's Amson Byington and William H. French, Morristown's Rev. Reuben Baker, John Gleed, and Hon. John West, to Johnson's A. W. Caldwell and Jonathan Dodge, to Waterville's J. M. Hotchkiss.

From its founding in the early 1800's to its termination with the end of the Civil War, the network of Underground Railroads provided that treacherous journey from slavery to freedom for many thousands of blacks. Its organization and operation were a mute and glorious conspiracy that, by defying federal fugitive slave laws, served the ideals of freedom and unity which are emblazoned on Vermont's seal and engraved in the character of her citizens.

The Civil War Muster of Vermont Blacks

At the entry of West Windsor's Mary L. Blood Memorial Library is a bronze tablet listing the 101 townsmen who served in the Civil War. Two were blacks. They were Privates Thomas Little, age twenty-six, and Abel Prince, age thirty-five. It is likely that they were fugitive slaves who, tired of their long, perilous escape to freedom via Vermont's Underground Railroad, had ended their journey at West Windsor's "station," and had settled in the town where both worked as farm laborers. Private Little enlisted on July 20, 1862, followed five days later by Private Prince, who had enlisted as a substitute. Note the year, for not until nearly a year and a half after the war's start were blacks given the right to fight for their own freedom in the ranks of the Union forces, although only in segregated units.

Opposition to military integration was particularly strong among citizens from the border states, as well as from northern soldiers. Besides the fear of insurrection, the racial hostility that lurked in the ranks was thought to be a threat to "the good order and morale" of the white men-in-arms. Yet there were also many whites in the northern states who believed that freed blacks should share the burden of waging war. (Ironically, in Louisiana and Tennessee the Confederate Army had earlier absorbed units of free blacks into its forces.) From the onset of the war, however, both fugitive slaves and freed ones had worked for the military as teamsters, mechanics, messboys, servants, maintenance personnel, and common laborers.

The policy of exclusion was eventually reversed by the reality of military necessity. But it was not until late July, 1862, that black enlistments on a trial basis were authorized by President Lincoln. Such enlistments proved so successful that thereafter voluntary service was actually sought, especially after Lincoln had issued the Emancipation Proclamation. The response was enthusiastic, so much so that by the close of 1862 four black regiments augmented the Union forces. The first of these, later known as Louisiana's "First Regiment Infantry Corps d'Afrique," was given its combat orders in September of 1862 by the Union's Gen. Benjamin F. Butler. By the war's end, 178,975 blacks had served in the federal forces. Of Vermont's total contribution of 34,238 men to the Union forces, 154 were black volunteers. They came from some fifty-seven communities.

"United States Colored Troops," designated as U.S.C.T.'s, served in segregated regiments under white officers. However, by the war's end, some seventy-five blacks had entered the ranks of the Union forces' commissioned officers. Massachusetts had commissioned ten; New Hampshire, two; and Vermont, none.

Segregation, however, was maintained even to the grave. Black veteran John Broadwell of Rutland, who had been killed in action, was buried not in Rutland's Grand Army lot along with his white fellow casualties, but in a remote section of the cemetery. Nearly one hundred years later, Rutland's Veterans' Council had Private Broadwell's remains exhumed and reburied with full military honors in the Grand Army section.

Inevitably segregation caused inequities. Until 1864 black servicemen were paid less than whites of the same rank. Historian Carter Woodson stated, "An entire regiment of Negroes had mastered techniques of peaceful protest by refusing to accept discriminatory wages, choosing instead to serve without pay for a year to demonstrate their devotion to their country."

Unequal pay was only one of the inequities, humiliations, and deprivations suffered by black servicemen. They were also given more arduous duty assignments, and had to enter combat "with a minimum of preparation and the poorest equipment." When captured, the Confederates treated them not as prisoners of war but as insurrectionary slaves. Many prisoners were killed outright. Many were sold as slaves. Others were killed "as an example to their race." Some were especially vulnerable to capture because they had served as spies and scouts whose familiarity with the South and ability to pass as local slaves were invaluable in guiding federal troops through unfamiliar territory and piloting Union gunboats through unknown waters.

The practice of segregating black troops from white units accounts for the fact that Privates Thomas Little and Abel Prince were not permitted to join any of the twelve regiments of Vermont Volunteers with their fellow West Windsor townsmen. Nor did they join the 1st, 41st, 43rd, or 45th U. S. Colored Troops, which absorbed most of the 154 black Vermonters who fought for the Union, perhaps because the quotas for these outfits had been fully met. Instead each journeyed alone to Boston where they met five days later to enlist in the heroic Fifty-Fourth Massachusetts Regiment, a unit of all-black volunteers. Private Little was assigned to Company H, and Private Prince served in Company K.

Of those 154 black Vermonters who served in the Union forces, sixty-eight fought in the ranks of the famous Fifty-Fourth. Led by Boston's wealthy, aristocratic Col. Robert Gould Shaw, the regiment had distinguished—and nearly extinguished—itself in the valiant yet futile effort to capture Fort Wagner, South Carolina, a victory that would have resulted in the fall of Charleston. That assault, on July 18, 1863, cost the regiment its beloved Colonel Shaw. It was this regiment that had indeed "nobly refused to receive its pay until it had been made equal to that of whites," according to historian Woodson. It was said that during this standoff Colonel Shaw personally paid his troops' wages.

Private Thomas Little was wounded in action. He received an honorable discharge on May 29, 1865, and returned to West Windsor. Pvt. Abel Prince was mustered out of the service on August 20, 1865, with an honorable discharge, and he moved to St. Albans. These two friends who had sought freedom in the rural obscurity of West Windsor, along with the sixty-six other

Shaw Memorial, *by Augustus Saint-Gaudens, honoring Col. Robert Gould Shaw and the black volunteers who served in Massachusetts's 54th Regiment.*

black Vermont volunteers in Massachusetts's Fifty-Fourth Regiment, have been immortalized for their loyalty and valor in sculptor Augustus Saint-Gaudens's famous bas-relief depicting Col. Robert Gould Shaw leading his troops. The monument faces the golden-domed statehouse atop Boston's Beacon Hill.

Diagonally across from it is another monument, a statue of Mary Dyer who as a Quaker was a member of another minority. She was hanged on Boston Common in 1660 for also espousing freedom, the freedom of speech and conscience. A victim of prejudice, she was a martyr to freedom, as were Privates Little and Prince and their fellow black Vermonters who had served in the Civil War, and who mostly remain unnamed—but not unsung.

The Public Saga of Private Scott

The roster of Vermonters who illuminate our history—like Ethan Allen, Chester Arthur, Calvin Coolidge, Stephen Douglas, and Joseph Smith—should include young Pvt. William Scott.

His imprint on his times merited no Medal of Honor as did St. Johnsbury's fourteen-year-old Willie Johnson, or the town of Johnson's sixteen-year-old Julian Scott (no relative), both of whom served heroically as drummer boys in the Civil War. Pvt. William Scott suffered his moment of destiny before his brigade, which early on Monday morning, September 9, 1861, had been mustered to witness his execution by a firing squad.

What route—what circumstances—led Private Scott to that day of reckoning?

Just two months earlier, on July 10, he had set out from Groton, Vermont, to enlist at Montpelier. He was twenty-two. His father, Thomas, was a farmer who had emigrated from Scotland in 1825. The Scotts had six sons and one daughter. Of the five sons who had volunteered for duty, David, George, John, Joseph, and William, the eldest, only two were to survive. Such was the family's awesome commitment to the Union cause from the state that had furnished more volunteers per capita than any other state.

Private Scott was assigned to Company K, Third Regiment of

Vermont Volunteers under the command of Brigadier General William "Baldy" Smith. After brief but intense training, the regiment hurried south and encamped near Chain Bridge outside Washington, D. C. The position was a strategic site on the approach to Washington from Virginia, and the regiment's primary function was to protect the capital. There, early in the morning of August 31, Pvt. William Scott was found asleep at his post. He was promptly court-martialed for dereliction of duty.

The charge: Violation of the 46th Article of War.

The specification: That Pvt. William Scott of Company K, Third Vermont Volunteers, "being a regularly posted sentinel did go to sleep upon his post; this at the hour before 3 and 4 A.M. on the 31st day of August 1861, while on picket guard, near Camp Lyon, D.C."

The verdict: Guilty.

The sentence: Death by firing squad.

What ensued made history. So popular was Private Scott with both his fellow enlisted men and officers that a petition for presidential clemency was signed by 191 members of Company K's soldiers and officers, including General "Baldy" Smith. Capt. Francis V. Randall, a Montpelier attorney, claimed in his widely read account of the incident that not only did "all the officers in the camp petition the president to pardon him," but he confirmed the fact that Private Scott "had stood sentry the night before for a sick mess-mate." A delegation headed by Brigade Chaplain Parmell presented the petition to President Lincoln's staff member, L. E. Chittenden of Vermont. He immediately arranged a meeting with the president.

General George McClellan reported in a letter to his wife, dated Sunday, September 8, the day before the scheduled execution, that "Mr. Lincoln came this morning to ask me to pardon a man that I had ordered to be shot." The tone of the comment reflects if not his dislike of the president, then his resentment for Mr. Lincoln's "interference."

Captain Randall's account added another detail, one that revealed both President Lincoln's lack of rapport with General McClellan, and his great compassion. Pvt. William Scott was imprisoned about eight miles from Washington. A temporary telegraph line connected the post with the president's headquarters.

When Lincoln received no acknowledgment of his order to stay the execution, scheduled for early the next morning, he suspected that it may not have been received. Therefore at ten o'clock that night the president traveled to the army post and, to the surprise of the sentries and the duty officers at headquarters, he delivered the order in person.

However, in compliance with President Lincoln's request, General McClellan had already secretly rescinded Private Scott's death sentence, but only after he had ordered a full-dress brigade muster to impress upon the troops the imperative for obedience to orders and the price to be paid for violating them. The regiments were assembled on the parade ground, "to form a hollow square" presumably to witness Private Scott's execution. The firing squad faced the prisoner. The death sentence was read. The drummers beat the traditional tatoo. Then instead of the order to fire, the president's pardon was read. It ended with the declaration that Pvt. William Scott was "to be released from confinement and returned to duty." The troops were reported to have cheered wildly.

Northern newspapers prominently heralded the pardon. Members of the brigade were interviewed. A diary entry of St. Johnsbury's Henry Herrick, a drummer in the Third Regiment's band, said "Bully for the president! But he could hardly have done otherwise under the circumstances. Scott had been guard several nights, and the night when he was found asleep had volunteered in place of a comrade who was sick."

Thomas Scott journeyed to Washington to thank President Lincoln for sparing his son's life. When Lincoln heard that five of his sons were in the service, he arranged for Scott to visit them.

Seven months later, on March 18, 1862, in a letter to a Groton, Vermont, friend, William Scott wrote nostalgically of his Vermont life. "I should like to be home this spring to get some new [maple] sugar to eat, but I think that we shall be home before a great while." Perhaps his homesickness was also sharpened by the memory of swimming in the Wells River's secluded pools or in Ricker's Pond, and of dances at the popular potluck "kitchen junkets."

The war there in Virginia was indeed a world away from the

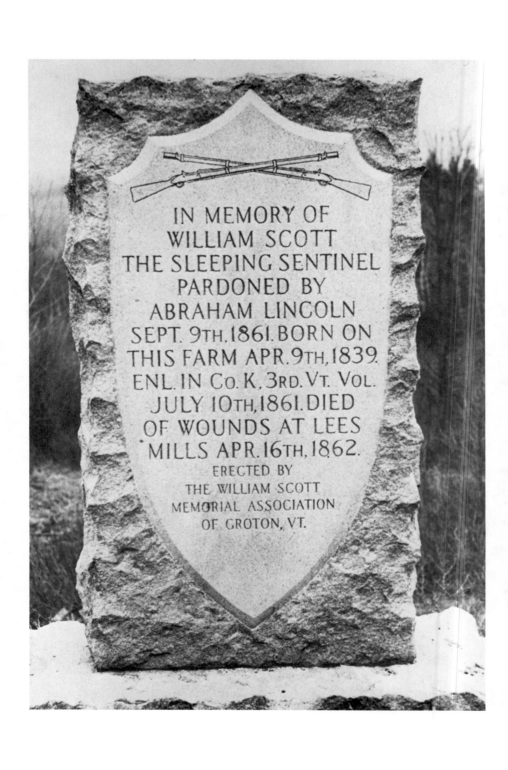

IN MEMORY OF
WILLIAM SCOTT
THE SLEEPING SENTINEL
PARDONED BY
ABRAHAM LINCOLN
SEPT. 9TH, 1861. BORN ON
THIS FARM APR. 9TH, 1839,
ENL. IN Co. K, 3RD. VT. VOL.
JULY 10TH, 1861. DIED
OF WOUNDS AT LEES
MILLS APR. 16TH, 1862.
ERECTED BY
THE WILLIAM SCOTT
MEMORIAL ASSOCIATION
OF GROTON, VT.

family's Vermont hill farm, a world he was never to see again. For on Sunday, five days after he had written to his friend, his outfit boarded transports at Alexandria and steamed down the Potomac River into Chesapeake Bay to Hampton. There it regrouped to organize its assault on Richmond in what was called the Peninsula Campaign. On April 10, Capt. Samuel Pingree (later a governor of Vermont) led the Vermont Volunteers against Confederate emplacements along the Warwick River at Lee's Mill. In the charge that opened the battle of Lee's Mill, Pvt. William Scott was shot. The next day he died, seven months after President Lincoln's pardon.

According to the *Philadelphia Inquirer's* war correspondent, "the first man who fell, with six bullets in his body, was William Scott of Company K." George Philbrick, a young soldier who also was from Groton, wrote three days later, "I saw where he was buried in a peach grove. The trees were all blossomed out, and it was a beautiful place."

The Rebels Are Here!

Truth can be stranger than a grade-B movie scenario, especially when the plot (with a cast of four thousand, which was the population of St. Albans, plus twenty-two genuine rebels) involved the conquest of a Vermont town by disguised Confederate soldiers. After only some twenty minutes of a typical Hollywood shoot-out, those rebel villains reduced that stronghold of Yankee tranquility to a town held hostage.

A scenario of that tragicomic raid will bring into sharper focus a picture of an oft-told melodrama:

TIME. The attack began at 3:00 P.M. on Wednesday, October 19, 1864. Wednesday was preferable to Tuesday, which was market day when too many people would be about. Wednesday would be quiet, particularly because about forty of St. Albans's prominent citizens, those most likely to exercise leadership in a crisis, were either in Burlington attending the Supreme Court's docket of important cases or at Montpelier's legislative session. Even the weather conspired to aid the raiders. A solid drizzle, like a musical accompaniment, struck a somber note. It was a prelude to trouble.

PLACE. St. Albans was chosen because it was the largest town nearest to Canada. Its location made it convenient for the invaders' escape and for diplomatic sanctuary. Furthermore the size and prosperity of this farming community supported three banks, all on Main Street: the First National Bank, the Franklin County Bank, and the St. Albans Bank, each of which the rebels planned to empty; and there were three hotels: the American, the St. Albans House and the Tremont. There the rebels had distributed themselves, the better to minimize their presence during the nine days that they had spent familiarizing themselves with the town and the banks' interiors.

CAST OF CHARACTERS. The good guys: St. Albans's citizenry. Some were foolhardy. Some were brave like bank teller Martin Seymour, Mr. Fuller of Fuller's Livery Stable, his competitor, Mr. Field, construction foreman Morrison, Collins Huntington who, although an old man, stood up totteringly for his rights (only to be knocked down). There was William Blaisdell who did not take kindly to bank robbers, even an armed one whom he tackled, and Captain Conger who took charge in the nick of time, but with poor results.

The bad guys: Confederates Daniel Butterworth, Alexander Bruce, the Reverend Cameron, Thomas Collins, James Doty, Samuel Gregg, Charles Higbie, William Hutchinson, Samuel Lackey, Joseph McGrorty, John McInnis, Dudley Moore, John Moss, Lewis Price, a Mr. Saunders, George Scott, Marcus Spurr, Charles Swager, Squire Teavis, Caleb Wallace, and their twenty-one-year-old leader, Lieutenant Bennett H. Young. None of the commandos was over twenty-six-years old, except McGrorty.

The raiders were not a motley gang of ruffians as was first believed. They were southern gentlemen, meaning they were well educated and from upper class families, even prominent ones. Caleb Wallace was Kentucky Senator John Crittenden's nephew. Another's uncle was former Vice President John C. Breckinridge. An unnamed twenty-second raider was rumored to have been Jefferson Davis himself.

PLOT.The raid had three objectives: to replenish the Confederacy's badly depleted coffers with the assets of St. Albans's three banks; to exact a token revenge for General Sheridan's devastation of the Shenandoah Valley by terrorizing the citizenry; and, by such terror, to force the Union army to rush troops north. By so doing, the pressure on the Confederate forces would be considerably relieved in those crucial sectors where the Union troops were advancing.

The action began on October 10 with the arrival from Canada of Lieutenant Young and two others. They registered at the Tremont Hotel. That same day two more conspirators checked into the American Hotel, while the next day three more settled in. They arrived by different routes and different means; some via the Montreal train, others by carriage from Burlington; some on horseback. On October 18 six came at different times of the day and put up at the St. Albans House. (It is doubtful that these southern gentlemen paid for their lodgings when they precipitously left on the 19th. Unlike tourists, they had not come to enrich the town.)

The rest arrived on the morning of the raid. Apparently all had extensive briefings on St. Albans's layout and especially the location and interiors of its three banks; the patterns of the citizens' daily activities, and the sites of the livery stables to decide which horses they would seize for their escape. Aristocratic Lieutenant Young even visited Governor Smith's mansion where he was given permission to admire the governor's fine stables for the same purpose. Some raiders tried unsuccessfully to rent rifles on the pretext of wanting to do some hunting. Their availability would determine whether the citizens were well supplied with guns. They were not.

Because of the variety of the rebels' clothes and their presence singularly or only in small groups, they did not attract attention, not even the Reverend Cameron whose evil intent was hidden by his clerical collar. Nor did the satchels that hung from their shoulders and in which they would tote their loot arouse curiosity. It was not unusual for travelers to carry such bags.

ACTION. The town hall clock's striking three was the raiders' signal for the simultaneous invasion of St. Albans's three banks on October 19. At the First National Bank, cashier Albert Sowles helplessly watched rebels Wallace, Doty, Bruce, and McGrorty seize the bank's assets. Another man present was old Gen. John Nason, deaf and senile. Whether he was a witness is doubtful because he sat by the window absorbed in his newspaper. Rebels McGrorty and Bruce, who first was posted at the door as a lookout, entered to hasten the heist. As the raiders were about to leave with stuffed pockets and satchels, in walked burly William Blaisdell. What, he asked Sowles, were these men up to? Sowles obliged him with the truth. Thereupon Blaisdell sprinted for the front door, but was blocked by a pistol-wielding rebel. Blaisdell jumped the man and pinned him to the floor. With their guns aimed at Blaisdell's head, two of the enemy demanded his unconditional surrender. The commotion distracted General Nason. On observing Blaisdell's plight, he declared "two upon one was not fair play." Convinced by the logic of futility, Blaisdell relinquished his untenable advantage. He was escorted to the town green which had become a well-guarded collection center for the rebels' prisoners.

Meanwhile at the Franklin County Bank, rebel Hutchinson had entered with four other conspirators. He asked cashier Marcus Beardsley what was the current cost of gold. Beardsley replied that he did not know, that the bank did not trade in gold. A sawyer, Jackson Clark, was there as was James Saxe who was seated by the stove. Then, when Saxe left, four more Confederates entered. Only then did cashier Beardsley detect their purpose as they silently advanced upon him, one with a long-barreled revolver poised to shatter his skull. At that moment in came a Mr. Armington to make a deposit. His arrival afforded the cashier a brief respite. But when Mr. Armington left, rebel Hutchinson declared almost in a whisper, "We are Confederate soldiers. There are a hundred of us. We have come to rob your bank and burn your town." Rob it they did, but not before Clark, who had been busy trying to look inconspicuous, raced for the door. He was seized and thrust into the vault along with Beardsley. The iron door was slammed shut. However, less than twenty minutes after the raiders had left, Armington returned. He heard voices from within the vault and, given the combination, he released the two in time for them to see the rebels galloping north with $76,000 of the bank's funds. The robbery had taken less than fifteen minutes.

Meanwhile at the St. Albans Bank, tellers Bishop and Seymour were confronted by rebels Collins, Price, Spurr, and Teavis. Two of them aimed pistols at their heads. One calmly announced, "Not a word. We are Confederate soldiers. We've come to take your town. We have a large force. We shall take your money, and if you resist, we will blow your brains out. We are going to do by you as Sheridan has been doing by us in the Shenandoah Valley."

Mr. Seymour tactfully argued that if their confiscation of private funds was indeed an act of war, then should he not inventory their take so that after hostilities were over, a claim for restitution could be made and honored? Rebel Collins won the rebuttal solely on the merits of his pistol's lethal potentiality. Thereupon the others quickly emptied the cash drawers and money from the safe into their valises and pockets. They overlooked $9,000 in a concealed drawer under a counter. Bags of silver worth $1500 were found, but except for $400, it was too heavy to tote. Merchant Samuel Breck entered to pay off a $393 note. A raider's cocked pistol persuaded him to deposit it with them. Mr. Breck was followed by Mr. Roach, a young store clerk who was to have deposited $210 of his boss's money. It, too, was seized. All four were herded into the director's room.

Except for the cash and about a hundred dollars in bonds, no gold was found. However, $50,000 in U. S. bonds stored in the vault and packaged in envelopes that belonged to the bank's customers were saved from the rapacious rebels by Mr. Seymour's coolness. In their haste, the raiders also missed $50,000 in signed sheets of St. Albans bank notes. According to historian L. L. Dutcher's account, written shortly after the raid, "It seems that they actually left behind more money than they took from the bank." This robbery lasted not more than twelve minutes.

All pedestrians who had appeared on or near Main Street were ordered to the green. When old, highly esteemed Collins Huntington, who was unaware that Confederates were terrorizing St. Albans, was told to "cross over to the green," he ignored the order. He thought the speaker was either daft or drunk. "If you don't go over," said the rebel, "I'll shoot you." Mr. Huntington replied, "Oh no, I guess you *won't* shoot me." He had guessed wrong. The bullet was deflected by a rib. It was a bad wound, but not fatal.

Some of the raiders began a roundup of horses for their escape. Owner Fields of Fields Livery Stable so vigorously opposed the theft of his horses that Lieutenant Young fired at him. The shot merely ventilated his hat, but it liberated his horses. A more serious casualty was Leonard Bingham. Knuckle-fisted and unarmed, he tried to unseat Lieutenant Young who had just taken his horse. He was shot in the stomach but survived. Lieutenant Young proceeded to dash about declaring "I take possession of this town in the name of the Confederate States of America," warning the people off the streets or onto the green, and shouting orders to his men to ignite wooden buildings with the grenade-size bottles of "green fire," a phosphoric compound that was part of their ammunition. These nineteenth-century Molotov cocktails, however, caused little damage, as much because of poor marksmanship as because of the rain. We are told that the rebels even failed to destroy the American Hotel's water closet which suffered little damage, "as the woodwork was kept wet."

Seven more horses were taken from Fuller's Livery Stable just as Mr. Fuller returned from out-of-town. At gunpoint, Lieutenant Young ordered him to fetch some spurs from Bedard's saddle shop, from which the rebels had earlier helped themselves to saddles and bridles. Fuller raced through Bedard's to alert the construction gang at the Welden House. The contractor, Elinus Morrison, of Manchester, New Hampshire, summoned his workers to accompany him and Fuller to the *Messenger* (wireless) office. By now word of the Confederate invasion was widespread. The rebels were mounted and were shooting wildly. An elm tree shielded Fuller from Lieutenant Young's fusillade. Morrison took advantage of Young's momentary diversion to seek refuge in Miss Beattie's hat shop. He only got to the door. Lieutenant Young's two shots struck Morrison in the abdomen. Two days later he died. His death was the only casualty.

One near-fatal oversight by Lieutenant Young was his failure to have first silenced the telegraph office in the depot. The operator's alert that "a body of rebels were in St. Albans plundering the banks, setting fire to the town, and shooting down citizens in the streets" caused the bells of Burlington to summon armed citizens. Five hundred immediately entrained for St. Albans. In anticipation of further Confederate incursions, the governor dispatched two companies of U. S. Veteran Corps. They arrived by sunup the next morning. In addition, one company of horse guards was convened, and a cavalry company mustered for duty.

An increasing number of armed St. Albanites were organized into immediate pursuit by cavalry captain George Conger. Their appearance spurred the rebels' retreat toward Canada, not, however, before Wilder Gilson coolly aimed at the last retreating raider, fired and shot rebel Higbie. Although badly wounded, he was taken to Quebec where he eventually recovered.

The Confederates advanced to Sheldon, pursued by Captain Conger's fifty hard-riding Vermonters. As there was not time to rob Sheldon's bank, which was closed, they rode on to Enosburg and thence into Canada. Thirteen of the rebels were arrested by Canadian authorities. Only William Teavis, who escaped dressed as a woman, managed to return to the South with the money he had stolen. About $88,000 of the loot was confiscated. The rebels' trial was long and costly both to St. Albans's banks and to the United States government in its effort to extradite the Confederate looters. On December 13 the judge ruled that the crime was beyond the court's jurisdiction. The raid was an act of war between the two belligerents. Extradition was denied. The judge ordered the defendants freed and the money returned to them. The crowds cheered. For like the British government, many Canadians were sympathetic to the Confederacy.

That was not the end of it. An effort was made to seek the extradition of some five rebels who had escaped the first trial. They appeared before Justice Smith at Montreal. He also denied extradition. Yet in later years the Canadian government, in the person of Governor-General Lord Monct, proposed to Parliament that $50,000 in gold should compensate St. Albans's banks for the equivalent of the $88,000 cash taken from the captured rebels which the court had returned to them. Parliament concurred. A later tally showed that the grand total of the rebels' robbery was $208,000. Therefore the net loss was $120,000 plus the $20,000 cost of their arrest and legal fees.

Meanwhile, back in St. Albans the alert to prevent further Confederate incursions from Canada into Vermont continued well into December. Major General Dix empowered all officers to order the troops quartered throughout northern Vermont "to shoot down the marauders" in case of any further attempted depredations, and to prevent by force their escape to Canada. The order had a sobering effect on Canadians sympathetic to the Confederate cause. It rendered Canada off-limits for the launching of rebel attacks on Vermont territory, a feat which the preposterous St. Albans raid had proved was feasible.

Women's Liberation — Vermont Style

In an earlier Vermont, women's liberation began at the grave.

The tombstone of Mrs. Eunice Page of Plainfield, Vermont, who died in 1888, aged seventy-three, had her disenchantment with her woman's lot recorded in this epitaph:

> Five times five years I lived a virgin's life.
> Nine times five years I lived a virtuous wife;
> Wearied of this mortal strife, I rest.

Her tally leaves the last three years unaccounted for. Obviously she derived no solace or peace from them. Not even in old age could Eunice Page have escaped her status as a woman. For male chauvinism was as deeply rooted in Vermont as are its sugar maples.

So pervasive was male chauvinism in the lives of Vermont women that evidence of it—in one word—was engraved on many tombstones. That word was *relict*. It means widow. Yet it had a different connotation. No belittlement is inferred in "widow," but a subtle disparagement is implicit in "relict." The fact that "relict" was sometimes preferred suggests that the prevailing attitude toward women, conditioned by female subservience, thus demeaned them with the stigma of inferiority.

This contention is supported by the fact that tombstones of married women, widowed or not, never recorded their maiden names. As their husbands' vassals, even in death, women were deprived of their family origins and thus of their familial identity. Note this typical example from a Brattleboro cemetery:

Experiance [*sic*]
relict of Samuel Wellington
died Dec. 17, 1838
AE 69
Her first husband
was Elias Bemis

Although twice a relict, the erstwhile Mrs. Wellington was deprived of her baptismal maiden name. Only Messrs. Bemis and Wellington's successive claim to her was heralded in the graveyard's elegy of fate.

Also chronicled on native slate, granite, or marble markers that cluster about the family monument is the sad evidence of women's long and active childbearing years. The appalling toll from epidemics of smallpox, measles, diptheria, scarlet fever, and from tuberculosis is mute testimony of recurring grief.

Yet disillusionment was not the typical daily fare of Vermont women. They were too busy to despair. The rigors of the environment imposed the challenge to survive. It fostered the stamina, courage, and resourcefulness necessary to cope. Coping was indeed the imperative for survival. In that spirit, a reverence for life, desite its discipline of hardships, echoes from a Sheddsville Cemetery stone inscribed:

Mrs. Rachael, Relict of Capt. Geo. Stow
died April 4, 1830. Age 51 years.
"No depth of earth, no sable bier
Nor death shall hold me captive here;
When life, that moved my being first,
Again reanimates my dust."

As for the living: A fine example of coping is offered by a Mrs. Williamson of Hartland. The diary of that industrious nineteenth-century farmwife states that she "made a fire, mended pants, set the breakfast going, skimmed 10 pans of milk, washed the pans, ate breakfast, went to the barn and milked 2 cows, brought the cream out of the cellar, churned 15 lbs. of butter, made 4 apple pies, 2 mince pies and 1 custard pie. Done up the sink, all done at nine o'clock." (What Mr. Williamson was doing during this period was not revealed.)

History, however, pays no homage to the accomplishments of such ordinary farmwives as Mrs. Williamson, despite the treadmill diligence of their admirable labors. In the chronicle of women's liberation it is the extraordinary lives of some Vermont women that made significant historical imprints.

Extraordinary indeed was Ann Story to whom women's liberation came suddenly and unbidden. For one September day in 1774 her husband Amos was killed. He had left Rutland to build a log cabin in the wilderness of Salisbury in Addison County. He had obtained land rights to one hundred acres there provided that his family would settle on it. Fourteen-year-old Solomon, his eldest son, had accompanied him. The house was nearly completed, the land nearly cleared when Amos was killed by a falling sugar maple. Undaunted, Ann, her three sons, and two daughters went to Salisbury in the spring and transformed the clearing into a farm in time to claim the deed.

Ann Story was born Hannah Reynolds. A no-nonsense woman who did not take kindly to frippery, she saw no reason to use a two-syllable Christian name when one would suffice. Thus Hannah became Ann. Yet her children were named Solomon, Ephriam, Samuel, Hannah, and Susannah, perhaps at her husband's insistence. She was very tall, sturdy, and vigorous; intelligent and compassionate; and so adept with axe and rifle, and at log-rolling, farm labor, and all such survival skills that "few men possessed such resolution, firmness and fearlessness as she."

All during the Revolutionary War Ann Story's fearlessness was frequently tested. Because she was a loyal Whig and actively supported the insurrectionists, her humble cabin was a refuge for enemies of the Royalists. The imminence of Indian raids, incited by the Tories, was a constant danger.

One spring day in 1776, a band of Indians, traveling cross-country, stopped to plunder all the houses in the area which they then set afire, including the Story farmstead. Not, however, as Ann Story wrote, "until we had secured our most valuable articles of household goods, and safely deposited them in our canoe,

which lay at the water's edge but a few steps from our door. Un-
observed by the Indians, we . . . were soon fairly out of their reach
in the deep water of the swamp. . . . We stationed ourselves back
in the swamp . . . where we could observe their movements and
make sure the hour and direction of their departure. Here we saw
Mr. Graves' house and our own burn at the hand of our cruel foe."

Ann Story lost no time in constructing a new house on the
same site. Other settlers sought safety elsewhere, but she could
not be dissuaded from staying. For the safety of her children,
however, widow Story resorted to an ingenious stratagem. Into
the opposite bank of Otter Creek, across from their cabin, they
dug a cavern large enough for them to spend the night. She wrote
that "the passage at the mouth of the cave was sufficient only to
admit our canoe so that all must lie prostrate in passing either in
or out. . . . The place where we slept was higher ground. . . . We
took the precaution to cut and stick down bushes at the mouth
of the cave, both when we were in and out of it, so that the place
of entrance would appear like the rest of the bank, and thus prevent discovery."

Despite her precautions, their hideaway was discovered. Compassion had betrayed her. Some Indians, who were herding their
white captives on their trek north, abandoned a woman who, because of her advanced pregnancy, could not keep up. Left to fend
for herself, she fortunately found Ann Story's cabin. There the
baby was born. Unfortunately for the family, their cave was likely
to be revealed by the infant's squalling. It was. At dawn one
morning, Ezekiel Jenny, a militant Tory, was strolling along the
riverbank when he heard the baby crying. He stopped. Soon Ann
Story's canoe emerged from its hidden cove with its telltale load.
Tory Jenny waited until she had paddled the sixty or so rods to
her landing. When he confronted her and demanded information
about the Whigs' whereabouts, she gave such noncommittal replies
that, she said, "He threatened to shoot me upon the spot, but to
all this I bid defiance, and told him I had no fears of being shot
by so consumate [sic] a coward as he . . . and I lost no time in
notifying Foot and Bentley [fellow Whigs] that Tories were within our borders; and immediately all the Whigs who could be raised
were set upon their track, and overtook them the same day in

Monkton, and that night captured every one of them, to the number of about twenty, and delivered them up to our authorities at Ticonderoga."

On returning to her cabin one day, Ann Story found the door secured from the inside. Some Yorkers soon came to the cabin. She shrewdly surmised that whoever was hiding within was not one of those hated New York Tories. She greeted the unwelcome visitors civilly. They pressed her to say who was behind that door. She merely smiled and assured them that the cabin was always locked to protect the children and herself, of course, from Indians or wild animals. If the Yorkers would like to come in, they were welcome to enter as she does, and she pointed to the roof. The Yorkers declined to follow, and left. But aware that they were watching her, she clambered to the roof, lifted a section of roof bark, then dropped to the floor. Not unexpectedly she was warmly greeted by a contingent of Green Mountain Boys.

Relict Ann Story became Mrs. Benjamin Smalley in 1792. Widowed again, she then married Capt. Stephen Goodrich, a Revolutionary War hero. She died on April 5, 1815, at the age of eighty-two.

Compassion had nearly defeated Ann Story. Anna Hunt Marsh made a cause of hers. In 1758 her parents had migrated from Massachusetts to Vernon, Vermont, where she was born in 1769. Her husband, Dr. Perley Marsh, was a member of a group of doctors committed to the welfare of the insane.

Their intentions were far more admirable than their treatment was efficacious, for they tried by submerging patients in ice-cold water for three or four minutes to suspend their consciousness and then resuscitate them. It was, in fact, torture in the guise of treatment. The failure of the experiment alerted Mrs. Marsh to the shocking conditions endured by mental patients. She was so appalled that she became a pioneer in the then revolutionary movement to liberate mental patients from the neglect and degradation suffered in their confinement.

On her death, at ninety-five, her will revealed a largesse that reflected her compassion, for the $10,000 she had left to fund a mental hospital created one of the United States' earliest mental hospitals. Called the Vermont Asylum for the Insane, it was in-corporated by the Vermont legislature in 1834. The hospital opened with twenty patients and a staff. Now it is the Brattleboro Retreat. Besides an in-patient capacity of six hundred, the Retreat has six diverse service, welfare, and research units.

Thus Anna Marsh's legacy of compassion effected the liberation of thousands from the tyranny of indifference.

A roster of crusaders for female liberty and equality must in-clude the name of Clarina Howard Nichols. The West Towns-hendite was, in fact, one of the nation's earliest prime movers for women's rights. In 1843 after thirteen years of marriage, she fostered her own rights by divorcing Justin Carpenter, a Baptist minister. They had three children. That same year she married George Nichols, publisher of the *Windham County Democrat,* for whom she had worked as the newspaper's editor.

Her editorials challenged a legal system that prevented women from "the ownership or enjoyment of the benefits of property." Aroused by her campaign, Senator Larkin Mead sponsored legis-lation to give Vermont matrons the right to own, inherit, manage, and bequeath property. Her lobbying, via her eloquent diatribes, resulted in additional legislation permitting women to make joint property ownership legal, to insure their husbands' lives, and to secure widows' inheritance rights.

Her campaigns led to her 1849 advocacy of women's suffrage. It was a cause that she championed before the Vermont legislature. Mrs. Nichols confronted the lawmakers with a petition and de-clared, "Having failed to secure her legal rights by reason of her disfranchisement, a woman must look to the ballot for self-pro-tection." That was in 1852. (The bill failed to pass but it was re-introduced twenty-eight years later and passed.)

One good cause deserves another. As her fame spread well be-yond Vermont, Mrs. Nichols also joined the temperance move-ment, and traveled widely promoting reform. Her disappointment in Vermont's 1852 rejection of women's suffrage sent her to Kansas's more fertile fields for sowing the seeds of women's rights. There she became an abolitionist.

Her husband died in 1855. In 1857 she became an editor of a

radical journal of the Free-Staters. She continued to campaign for women's rights in Kansas, Wisconsin, and Ohio. The Civil War drew her to Washington in 1863 where she and Birsha, her daughter, lived until 1866. There she was a supervisor of the Home for Colored Orphans. But she again returned to Kansas a year later to lobby for a women's suffrage amendment then before the Kansas legislature. It failed to pass. Clarina Nichols died eighteen years later in California. She was seventy-five.

The dynamics of womanpower as exemplified by Ann Story, Anna Marsh, Clarina Nichols, and—yes—Hartland's Mrs. Williamson is a tribute to the courage, character, and devotion with which these Vermonters have enriched the family of man—and woman.

Rufus Streeter's Murderer

Was the question of who murdered Rufus Streeter really answered with the hanging of Asa Magoon on November 23, 1879?

Asa Magoon's descendants now populate many states. One branch had taken root in Missouri; and one member of the clan has raised that question in the hope of erasing from its genealogy the stigma of having an ancestor who had been hanged for murder. If sufficient evidence of Asa Magoon's alleged innocence could be exhumed from the crypt of history, or new evidence offered in the man's belated behalf, then it would justify a review that might exonerate Asa Magoon with a posthumous pardon.

One bit of questionable new evidence is an alleged deathbed confession to the crime. It was supposedly made nine years after Asa Magoon's execution by Hannah Perrin, who died in 1888 at the age of seventy-five. She had been sixty-two on the night of Rufus Streeter's murder on October 14, 1875, a fact which may—or may not—have compounded some of the crime's imponderables. She knew both men well; speculation about her familiarity with them raised some questions and some eyebrows.

Asa Magoon had lived with his wife in Topsham, Orange County. They had seven children: Charles, the eldest, who "bears a fair reputation"; Asa, Jr., "a man of bad repute" whose record (from 1880 to 1890) included two larceny charges, two charges for trespass, a liquor violation and, together with brother Silas, another indictment for larceny. There was Ernest, and Fred, a tax collector. Edson, the sixth son, had died in infancy. The seventh was their daughter Emily, who had two illegitimate children before becoming Mrs. Rufus Streeter, and who suddenly became his widow on that October night.

A prosecutor's eye-view of Asa Magoon saw a defendant who "has borne a hard character for many years and is suspected of having murdered two other persons, one a German peddler, who is said to have been last seen at his house and the family was afterwards in possession of goods believed to belong to the peddler. A house in which a Mrs. Bowen lived was burned at Corinth and her charred remains found . . . with the skull broken in. Magoon had been intimate with her, but sufficient proof could not be obtained to convict him. Later, Magoon was arrested for burning the buildings of his father-in-law, indicted by grand jury, but escaped a trial through a legal technicality. He had several times been arrested on criminal charges and once escaped to Canada," according to the *Free Press and Times*, October 23, 1879.

As for Hannah Perrin: From a dossier on the case (culled from newspaper accounts of the trial by historian Lee F. Perkins of Barre), the *Montpelier Daily Journal* of October 4, 1876, stated "As there is an evident tendency on the part of the defense to connect her with the crime, her testimony was very interesting. She is a genuine Irish woman, with a strong brogue and keen wit, and even searching cross-examination . . . failed to elicit even a hint of the dread secret which is supposed to be locked in her breast."

The trial began on October 5, 1876. Excerpts from the newspaper coverage state that Hannah Perrin, a widow, testified that Streeter and Magoon came to her place, a roadhouse known as the Spring House. They arrived at sunset on October 14 after having been to the Barre racetrack. "They were somewhat liquored up," she stated. She added that she gave Streeter a crab apple pie; that he and Magoon then had a dispute about a missing jug of rum during which Magoon threatened to kill him. Magoon stayed to look for the lost liquor while Streeter drove off toward Orange. Then Magoon soon followed "and she didn't see either of them again that night and knew nothing of the murder till informed early the next morning." Drs. Jackson and Bigelow, who did the postmortem, said Streeter's wounds "were simply terrible and sufficient to kill ten men. The condition of the undigested food in Streeter's stomach showed that he must have been killed not less than half an hour, or more than two hours, after eating the pie . . . . This goes strongly to support the government's theory that Magoon committed the murder almost immediately after leaving Mrs. Perrin's. . . . The defense, however, maintained that Streeter was not killed until ten or eleven o'clock; and that he [Streeter] remained behind at Mrs. Perrin's and let Magoon go home alone." In support of this theory, Mr. Heath, the defendant's lawyer, "will attempt to prove that digestion occurred much more slowly because of Streeter's continual intoxication; and that Mrs. Perrin had repeatedly threatened to have vengeance upon Streeter for leaving her. It seemed they used to live together . . . and marrying or pretending to marry, for he had another wife living in Barre, Magoon's daughter [Emily]."

On October 6 the state's attorney, Hon. W. P. Dillingham, presented the prosecution's evidence of their theory "that Magoon and Streeter had a quarrel at Hannah Perrin's, which had its origin in the loss of a jug of rum by Magoon; that Streeter got into the team, drove it into the road, with the avowed intention of going immediately home; that Magoon thereupon threatened his life, followed him to the spot in the road opposite where the body was found, split a rail from the fence, struck Streeter repeatedly over the head, and murdered him." It was suggested that Hannah Perrin, then aged sixty-two, could not have wielded such a cudgel with enough force to have crushed Streeter's skull. "The principal witnesses yesterday," according to the press, "were Mr. and Mrs. Romaine Bradbury, and Merrill Wilde, who witnessed this quarrel at Hannah Perrin's, and in addition Bradbury testified that he heard the blows struck."

On October 7 the *Montpelier Daily Journal* quoted defense attorney Heath as having said, "the facts that had been developed by the prosecution were substantially true." He would prove, however, that while at Hannah's "all three drank of this liquor which had been mentioned . . . and that a jug of rum was stolen from

Magoon, probably with the connivance of Streeter; that some sharp words took place between Hannah and Magoon about the theft; that he and Streeter then left in the team and proceeded as far as the watering trough, where Streeter got out and returned to Hannah's to pass the night, an old habit of his, which was the last Magoon ever saw of him alive."

The principal witnesses for the defense were Asa Magoon's sons, Asa, Jr. and Charles. Asa, Jr. testified to a fight he and Streeter had at Hannah's in March, 1875, in which Streeter hit Hannah over the head with a stick of wood, and Hannah, he claimed, "returned the compliment with interest, and finally turned them both outdoors at three o'clock in the morning." The reporter wrote that "Little Asa tried to account for the blood on the wagon by swearing that Streeter had a nosebleed while riding in it from West Topsham on the day before the murder."

In the defense's closing argument, Attorney Heath "discussed the scene at Hannah's, and claimed that if the grave would give up its dead, to tell the secrets of that awful night, she would be found to be the murderer, and *not* Magoon. He alluded to the threats, which the proof [evidence] tended to show she had repeatedly uttered against Streeter, and the continued friendship existing between Magoon and Streeter. . . . It was not an unnatural thing for Streeter to have left Magoon and gone back to Mrs. Perrin's," for, he declared, "they had often had drunken sprees together."

Part of the prosecution's summary stated not only that it was unlikely a woman could have bashed in Streeter's skull with such force that "the indentation in the ground showed that the body had fallen or been thrown from the wagon and that Streeter was last seen sitting in the wagon with Magoon by his side." He referred to Magoon's "ridiculous attempts to account for the blood on the wagon, leading lines and buffalo robe, by saying that he had killed a sheep and spattered the blood; and asserted that Magoon, and not Mrs. Perrin, was the one who had threatened to kill Streeter."

The trial ended on November 17. After three and one-half hours of deliberation, the jury found Asa Magoon guilty of murder in the first degree.

Among his last words, uttered from the scaffold, was an appeal for a stay of execution. "Give me one year to get a new trial," he pleaded, "and if the decision is against me after a fair hearing, I won't find a word of fault for being hung. I always knew Streeter well, kept him in spending money, fed him for eleven months and now to be killed for treating a man well, it ain't right [trembling violently and shedding tears]. It's unjust."

Prison records report that he was executed with the same noose "used in executing Ward, Kavanagh, Barnet, Welcomb, Miller, Gravelin, and Phair." None of Magoon's family had visited him in jail. Not until four days after his hanging did his widow write to the warden with a demand for his body.

Nine years after Magoon's hanging, it is said that Hannah Perrin made a deathbed confession that she had murdered Rufus Streeter. The only evidence is a scribbled diary entry of a woman who was present at Hannah's death in 1888. No substantiated evidence of the oral confession is obtainable. Instead of redemption, therefore, history can only accord Asa Magoon the immortality of doubt.

Perhaps Rufus Streeter's spirit has invoked a curse on the Magoons. According to Elinore Garcia of Burlington, (an aunt of Ernest Wilson, the ill-fated Asa Magoon's great-grandson), in 1979 or 1980 an Arnold Magoon was murdered in Brandon, Vermont. A few years earlier, Vermont serviceman Richard Magoon was murdered in Tennessee.

Alien Yankees

Perhaps it was the lack of transportation that prevented refugees Adam and Eve from emigrating to Vermont. Like the Garden of Eden, the Green Mountain State has an ample apple crop, and latter-day immigrants, for various reasons, have hailed it as God's country.

However, many of Vermont's pioneers thought differently. The earliest settlers found the environment too hostile, its earth too rocky, its natural resources too few, its topsoil too depleted by their ignorance of or indifference to crop rotation, and later by erosion from too much sheep-grazing. In short, those first settlers whose stake was in agriculture and stock-raising found Vermont so inhospitable that they abandoned their farmsteads to head west. They transplanted their Vermont way of life to Kansas, Michigan, and Ohio.

These Yankee pioneers were of Scotch and English stock. They had filtered into Vermont from New York and from the other New England states. As early as 1774, Scots settled in Barnet and Ryegate. Caledonia County got its name from Scottish pioneers who had bought 7,000 acres there. They applied their labor and hopes to the cultivation of the land, and exercised their compulsion for economic and political independence. Fortunately for Vermont, subsequent settlers were infected by the contagion of the pioneers' character. For regardless of their national origin and cultural diversity, the pioneer spirit gave the newcomers the will to survive. It was immunity against defeat.

The exodus of many Vermont Yankees got its impetus from two catastrophes. Both occurred in the same decade. The government's embargo on wool for British mills, imposed just before the regionally unpopular War of 1812, fleeced Vermont's sheep raisers of their largest, most profitable market. The drop in prices resulting from the glut of wool—in an age before federal price supports—caused a severe depression. The depression was also precipitated by floods, poor crops, epidemics; by foreclosures and bank failures.

Then in 1816 occurred "the summer of no summer." Starting on June 7, a heavy snowfall continued for three days. It foretold a prolonged freeze. Deprived of grain, hay, and grazing, quantities of livestock died. Sheep that already had been sheared froze to death. Farmers butchered their emaciated livestock to salvage the scant meat by salting it for those gloomy months ahead. The unripened corn was destroyed even before husks had sprouted, and the freezing temperatures caused other crop failures. Apple trees were literally "nipped in the bud." Nothing grew. Through the fall and winter the destitution worsened. So widespread were the privation and hunger that some towns (like Worcester, just north of Montpelier) were abandoned. Many families never returned. A by-product of the catastrophe was an influx of grain and food speculators. Like locusts, they fed on those destitute citizens who had stayed.

Why then did immigrants willingly become Vermont's new Yankees? With the sprawl of railroads, Vermont became more accessible. Labor was needed to extend their advance. Improved transportation, both by rail and road, was concomitant with an upswing of the state's economy caused by New England's industrial revolution. With ample waterpower, textile, lumber, paper, and flour mills abounded. An increased demand for high-quality marble and granite required skilled workers to tap the resources of the state's quarries. Industrial and agricultural technology, abetted by numerous inventions by Vermonters, needed regiments of workers to meet the demands of an ever-expanding market for consumer goods and services. The invention of agricultural machinery plus new farming techniques and cheap land also attracted Europeans fleeing poverty and famine, and who sought social and political equality and religious tolerance. One incentive for immigration was offered by Vermont's legislature. Like nature, the state government abhorred a vacuum. Therefore to replace its departed Yankee farmers, the legislature advertised abroad the availability of some 500,000 acres (about 10% of the state's arable land) "at $3.00 to $5.00 per acre."

Who were the state's latter-day Yankees—and why?

FRANCO-AMERICANS

Vert means green; *mont* means mountain. The origin of Vermont's name, therefore, underscores the influence of French-Canadian immigration. Consider, too, that Montpelier, the state's capital, was named after the French city, that Monsieur Champlain's name for La Rivière à la Moelle became the Lamoille River, that Grand Isle is French for Great Island, that Vergennes has its counterpart in France.

The first Frenchman to leave his imprint on Vermont was Samuel de Champlain. The lake so named honored his discovery of it in 1609. In 1666 the French established their first settlement at Isle La Motte. Before England's victory over France in 1760, the towns of Georgia, Highgate, Swanton, and St. Albans were French seigneuries (domains) with French names. When the Marquis de Lafayette arrived in Burlington in 1825 to lay the University of Vermont's cornerstone, among his greeters was a large contingent of French-Canadians. So prominent and populous were they in Burlington that in 1839 the first French-language newspaper in the United States, *Le Patriote Canadien,* was published there. Soon afterward St. Albans was to have one, too.

Because they resented their status as second-class citizens (imposed under British rule), and because of dire poverty at home, so many French-Canadians crossed the border that by 1850 they numbered 14,000. According to historian Cora Cheney, "Protestant Vermont was aghast at the influx of Roman Catholics ... but settled Vermonters accepted the new order with extraordinary decorum considering their anti-Catholic traditions," so much so that the anti-Catholic, anti-foreign Know-Nothing Party gained only a tenuous foothold. The press, "provoked by letters from thoughtful citizens, finally shamed the party out of Vermont."

The language barrier and their Catholicism made these early immigrants protectively clannish. Where possible, they established a benevolent society to assuage the pressure of poverty, a parish, and a French-language paper as the social and cultural nucleus of their self-contained enclaves. Burlington's St. Joseph parish, founded in 1850, was the country's first all-French parish. Its first bishop was Louis-Joseph de Goesbriand, a nobleman, after whom Burlington's municipal hospital was named. Throughout the state, twenty-three French-Canadian Catholic churches still flourish, although in only a few is French exclusively spoken. Winooski takes the lead as Vermont's predominantly French city. Of its 7,000 citizens, some 5,000 are Franco-Americans, and French is often spoken in its business establishments.

The Civil War opened a floodgate of immigration to Vermont. Some 40,000 French-Canadian New Englanders served in the Union Army. The 1900 census lists 55,000 Vermonters of French-Canadian extraction, and in 1958 there were between 65,000 and 100,000. The fact that many people had lost their French names through trans-cultural marriage or had adopted English names accounts for that imprecise tally.

IRISH-AMERICANS

Many Irish who came to Vermont in the late 1700's did so as indentured servants. Unmistakably Irish names in the federal census of 1790 and 1800 suggest that more sons of Erin were Vermonters than indicated in various county and town histories.

Matthew Lyon, a particularly flamboyant son of Ireland, acquired Ethan Allen's niece for his wife. He also had acquired three Congressional seats from three different states. His origins were humble and unpromising. When only fifteen, he had talked a ship's captain bound for America into taking him aboard as a white slave whose services would be partial payment for his passage. He had agreed that on his arrival in New York, he would "be sold at auction." He was. The price of sixty pounds was paid by a Litchfield, Connecticut, merchant. After purchasing his freedom three years later, his career grew progressively more dramatic. As one of the Green Mountain Boys, he helped sieze Fort Ticonderoga from its lethargic British commander. In 1783 he was one of Fair Haven's founders. There he grew prosperous from his iron and woolen mills, his publishing business, and (like the Allens) from land speculation. He was elected to Congress in 1796. Convicted vindictively and probably unfairly "of violating the Sedition Act," he won re-election from his "seat" in jail. The victory made him a militant champion of free speech. It was Lyon's single deciding vote in the 1800 election that put Thomas Jefferson in the White House.

The failure of his Fair Haven business ventures prompted him to emigrate to Kentucky. From 1803 to 1811 he served Kentucky as a congressman. Then, restless for new adventures, he moved to Arkansas Territory where in 1822 he again became a delegate to Congress, and established a record for having served three states as a congressman.

Matthew Lyon was typical of Vermont's Irish-Americans for his high-octane temperament and enterprise, for his social and political activism, his hatred of British colonialism, his contempt for racial prejudice, and for his beginnings as an indentured servant. Atypical of the majority of the Irish immigrants was Lyon's record of quick, dramatic social, business, and political success, and the lapse of his Catholicism.

Veterans of the War of 1812, lured by cheap land and the challenge of pioneering in new territory, left many of their Vermont towns for the West. They were replaced by Irish newcomers from New York and Quebec. Mostly farmers, they settled on the spreads vacated by the emigrated Yankees. Typical of this population flux was the revitalization of Fairfield. By 1830, the families of James Carroll, Peter Connelly, Patrick Deniver, Michael Hayes, Patrick King, Lawrence and Peter Kirk, and the McEnany brothers had practically made Fairfield an Irish-Catholic town whose spiritual guidance was provided by Father Jeremiah O'Callaghan, a popular missionary priest. The migratory flux continued. While there were over one hundred Irish-owned farms in Father O'Callaghan's parish, only some forty now remain. The Irish westward trek for new opportunities repeated the emigration pattern of their Yankee predecessors. The deserted cemetery of Underhill's Irish families attests to the same exodus from Vermont regardless of its green valleys and hills.

The need for laborers to feed the voracious growth of Vermont's railroads saved many Irishmen from the famine of 1846, caused by Ireland's blighted potato crop. They had long chafed under the yoke of British domination that doomed them to poverty. American advertisements for laborers sent them swarming to Montreal, where passage was cheaper, and to New York and Boston. Many were hired at dockside by Vermont labor contractors. Others followed when word of Vermont's verdant pastures reached home. There were 15,000 Irish in the state by 1850. They outnumbered the French-Canadians.

POLISH-AMERICANS

According to historian Helen Ankuda, most of Springfield's Polish and Russian immigrants came from the same locale. It was from that quadrant of eastern Poland that abuts Russia's western border. Their language "wasn't the language of the educated Polish or Russian people, but one that was common to both nationalities."

Springfield's first immigrants were two farm workers, Peter Kisler and Wasil Koledo. They arrived about 1890. Later, when they saved enough money for their young wives' passage, they settled down to family life. This was the typical pattern of importing their relatives. The immigrants' education had been meager. In their mother country, schools were attended briefly before spring planting and after the harvest. Religious training by the village priests was more regular, for the peasants were devout. In their Vermont homeland, the language problem was a particular handicap. Their poor education, unpronounceable names, lack of English, and even their "foreign" orthodoxy, as members of the Eastern Orthodox Church atop Parker Street Hill, initially isolated them. Thus assimilation was slow and difficult.

However, they proved to be hard workers who adapted well to the arduous, menial work at factories and mills like the John T.

Stack Company's Shoddy Mill, where they made the inferior-quality fabric from reclaimed wool. Woman workers labored six days a week from 7:00 A.M. to 6:00 P.M. for $8.00 per week. The more skillful workers progressed to the city's machine shops. Springfield's flourishing machine-tool industry in part owed both its growth and reputation for high-quality workmanship to its Polish and Russian-American Vermonters.

Bellows Falls also had a large Polish community whose members worked in the city's paper and woolen mills. Many immigrants accelerated their Americanization by learning English at night schools, and thus achieved better employment. It was a proud day for those families whose members traveled to Woodstock for their certificates of citizenship. Second generation Polish-Americans achieved economic security and acceptance as foremen, machinists, municipal employees, building-trade workers, entrepreneurs, politicans, and such professionals as teachers, social workers, nurses, doctors, and lawyers. Thus their new status admirably marked the transition from second-class citizenship, as people of recent foreign extraction, to full-fledged Vermonters.

SWEDISH-AMERICANS

Why did so many Swedes leave for a country whose seasons, climate, and scenery were so much like their homeland's? There were three reasons. From its beginning, the Swedish church was a national institution. Not only were birth and marriage records kept by the church rather than the state, but the state's tax lists were based on the church's roster of communicants. So close was the bond of church and state that the former was partly supported by public taxes.

In 1853 Swedish Lutheranism was jolted by the widespread withdrawal of three liberal, evangelical groups: The Swedish Methodists, Swedish Mission Friends, and the Swedish Baptists. Many of these apostates emigrated to America. Those defectors who came to Vermont were mostly the Mission Friends. The democratic character of Congregationalism particularly appealed to them, as did the financial assistance with which the Congregationalists welcomed them.

In addition to seeking religious freedom, they emigrated because several seasons of ruinous Swedish droughts caused such hunger that their scant flour reserves were extended with pulverized tree bark. Famine was endemic. Furthermore, the Swedes resented and resisted both the domination of the landed gentry and their oppressive, poorly paid work for the manufacturing and mining monopolies. As every action has its equal and opposite reaction, socialism and emigration followed. Between 1850 and 1900, over one million Swedes sought religious freedom, social justice, and economic betterment in America.

Meanwhile, back in Vermont, the legislature had appointed a commissioner, a Mr. Valentine, to propose countermeasures to replenish the agricultural workers who with other rural people had moved into the cities, or who, since the close of the Civil War, had heeded Congress's siren call to go west for tornadoes, locusts, and government lands at dirt-cheap prices. In fact some 175,000 native Vermonters, which was nearly half of the state's population, had emigrated. The labor pool was empty. On his trip west to Minnesota country, Commissioner Valentine discovered the hardworking, thrifty, well-educated, family-oriented Protestant Swedes. Even their native soil and environment was similar to Vermont's minus Sweden's long, sunless, and depressing winters.

Vermont therefore published a map with descriptions in Swedish and English of some sixty-two townships in ten counties, where farms with farm buildings "in fair shape" were available, dirt cheap. Inquiries poured in. The initial response rewarded Vermont with 554 Swedish families. Each township had organized welcoming committees to help the Swedes get settled. Nebraska's John Nordgren, a prosperous Swedish-American farmer, came to inspect Vermont's land offerings. He was so impressed by their potentiality that he went to Sweden in 1889 to recruit settlers. Sixty-five Swedes were the first newcomers. Seven families settled in Wilmington, thirteen in Weston, and the rest in Vershire. With them was their pastor. Grafton and Jamaica also benefited by later Swedish arrivals. In each community Commissioner Valentine provided the settlers with interpreters and free stationery and stamps. The towns' well-organized welcome included temporary housing and entertainment. The legislature recompensed Mr.

Nordgren "for four months' time and expenses amounting to a total of $1,250."

Those Swedes who shunned the rocky hill farms found work elsewhere in Vermont. Many chose logging, mill work, industrial labor, and quarrying. Proctor's marble center and the environs of Rutland had, and still have, the state's largest Swedish-American communities. While most of the men there did quarry-related work, the women "hired out" as domestics to augment the family's income. Brattleboro's Carpenter and Estey piano and organ companies partly owed their worldwide reputations for superior instruments to the fine craftsmanship of their Swedish workers. Smith Company's baby carriage factory also employed Swedish precision metal workers. Quincy, Massachusetts's long quarries strike in 1899 caused an influx of Swedish granite workers to Montpelier and Barre. By 1920, the twenty-year influx had brought some nine hundred Swedes to that area alone. Swedish enterprise matched their industriousness. At one time there were fifteen Swedish-owned granite quarries in Barre.

Although they gave Vermont no Swedish place names, the immigrants' legacy to their adopted state was their ethic of piety, civic responsibility, industriousness, and probity. It was a complement to Yankee character that, by fostering their acceptance, hastened their assimilation.

ITALIAN-AMERICANS

If a tourist were to visit Carrara, Italy, and reveal that he or she was from Vermont, it is likely that some of that famous marble center's *paesans* would eagerly ask whether he knew descendants of kinsmen named Andrei, Baldacci, the Bertagna brothers, and Fontana who in 1882 had settled in Barre and Proctor. Their arrival had been sponsored by Senator Redfield Proctor who was in Italy on business for his Vermont Marble Company, and who had persuaded them to come to Sutherland Falls (later named Proctor) to teach their art and establish their studios here.

The tradition of Italian craftsmanship has spanned the centuries from the Renaissance to contemporary Vermont. It is singularly evident in the Carrara connection. About 1504 Michaelangelo had journeyed there from Rome to select one perfect marble monolith from which to carve his Pietà that is now in the Vatican's Sistine Chapel. In Barre's Hope Cemetery—one of America's finest museums of memorial sculpture—is the Palmisano Monument's Pietà, an exquisite replica in Barre granite. It was designed by Al Comi and sculpted by Alcide Fautoni, both Vermonters.

Or would the Vermont tourist know any descendants of Elia Corti and Samuel Novelli who sculpted Barre's famous statue of poet Robert Burns? Or did they know any Abates, related to Carlo who had founded an art school there, or descendants of monument designer Joseph Aja and Guiliano Cechinelli, another famous Barre artisan?

The Italians' contribution to Vermont's beauty is apparent wherever imposing statues and monuments adorn municipal buildings, village greens, city parks, and cemeteries. For Italian quarry workers, masons, wood and stone carvers, and architects applied their skills and artistry with a touch of Renaissance grandeur. A unique model of such grandeur is former Governor Allen Fletcher's Bavarian castle in Proctorsville. Now the Castle Inn, it was built in 1901 of Vermont granite (from the governor's quarries) by Italian designers, masons, plaster sculptors, and wood and stone carvers. Surely this former citadel of Yankee prestige and wealth, created by Italian artisans, is one fitting example of the pluralism that now characterizes Vermont culture.

Even before the Italian artisans chose to carve a new life in the alien world of Vermont, they possessed such Yankee characteristics as resourcefulness, shrewdness, stamina, and resilience. Their strengths had been annealed on the forge of their history and environment. They were born survivors. Before 1860, when Italy first became a nation, the country was merely a geographical entity, a conglomeration of fiercely independent city-states, some of which were ruled by foreign powers. All existed in a maelstrom of political and economic chaos. This historic divisiveness resulted in the Italians' community—rather than nationalistic—orientation. Their community cohesiveness was an outgrowth of their strong family ties. The community became, indeed, their extended family. It was their refuge. Its durability was wrought by their familial cohesiveness, loyalty, and pride. That plus ability and hard work earned them their neighbors' respect, and contributed to their eventual success as entrepreneurs.

Many Italians had emigrated to Proctor from Westerly, Rhode Island, a declining granite center, and from Quincy, Massachusetts, whose quarry operations had been beset by strikes in the 1890's. Then in 1895 a political upheaval in Carrara resulted in a new wave of migration to Barre and Proctor. By 1918, Barre had become the largest granite center of the world, and about half of its population was of Italian extraction. The second generation of these Italian-Americans, many of whom were college graduates, had become tradesmen, restaurateurs, teachers, engineers, nurses, doctors, lawyers, municipal workers, labor leaders, and politicians. In 1957, nearly half of the city's municipal posts were in the hands of second-generation Italians, including the office of mayor.

Not all the Italian immigrants were from northern Italy's industrial and quarrying centers. A minority of southern Italians were initially employed in Vermont's booming railroad expansion. They settled mostly in Burlington, Montpelier, Rutland, Barre, and White River Junction. Many from the urban centers of the industrialized north who were not quarry workers or artisans, but whose families were business-oriented or who were landowners, came to seek independence through their respective business enterprises. The second generation of White River Junction's Guarino family exemplifies not merely successful assimilation, but a dynasty distinguished by careers in military and diplomatic service, in law, in education (both as teachers and administrators), in business, and in public service.

Vermonters of foreign extraction—the Scots, French-Canadians, Irish, Polish, Swedish, and Italians plus the few Germans, Hungarians, Swiss, and Spanish, too—all brought to Vermont the flavor of their respective cultures. Yet rather than dilute Vermont's Yankee character, these latter-day settlers enhanced it. The very essences of their disparate backgrounds were homogenized by assimilation, and became an integral part of Vermont life and culture as characteristically "Vermont" as her zesty cheddar cheese.

There's Fraud
in Them There Hills!

With the speed of a seismic tremor, California's gold-rush fever spread east to Vermont. Its "carriers" were Vermonters who, having recently returned from gold-panning there, started a local gold rush with the contagion of their zest for quick wealth. The epicenter of their claims was in the Bridgewater-Plymouth area.

Gold was indeed there. Matthew Kennedy, a Plymouth native who had prospected in California, found gold nuggets when he was intent only on fishing a tributary of Tyson's Echo Lake called Buffalo Brook. Kennedy had to share the claim of discovery with fellow townsman William Hankerson who in 1855 also found gold in Plymouth. Furthermore, geologists agreed that its purity "exceeded that generally found in California." Understandably neither man—nor other prospectors—wanted their discoveries known, and that included Bridgewater's "Arm" Weeden. (It is said that "he stored three ounces of gold in a Patoka Liver Pill Bottle" which, after his death, relatives had thrown out along with the accumulated junk of his cabin.)

Yet the sources of Vermont gold could not be concealed, especially when mining operations were involved. The largest, most productive of these was the famous Rooks Mining Company in Plymouth. Its stockholders got fat dividends until the mine was played out. Gold-rush fever ultimately subsided when prospectors and speculators discovered that "more money was poured into the ground than extracted from it."

So quite a few prospectors with depleted or otherwise worthless claims eagerly revealed their locations to out-of-state gold diggers and speculators in order to "mine" their gullibility and greed. Thus fraud became a lucrative by-product of Vermont gold-mining.

Historian Donald Campbell claimed: "There is considerable evidence that some of the farmers in the hill villages 'salted' the brooks flowing through their upland sheep pastures before selling them to gullible investors from 'down country'." One method of salting a pan of gravel "right under the eye of a city slicker" was for the tobacco-chewing panner merely to spit a glob of tobacco juice, mixed with gold dust, into the pan "for good luck"; and by thus convincing his prospect of the richness of his stream bed make his worthless claim profitable.

Another method of mine-salting was used so successfully in 1885 that the following news item appeared in the *Vermont Journal:*

Sheddsville Hills Were Prospected For Midas' Metal
West Windsor Finds Gold Near Saw Mill

February 5, 1887—About the first of October, 1885, Benjamin Warren and C. L. Fallon, farmers living in Sheddsville, near West Windsor, became convinced, through the representation of an old miner who could not resist to do a little prospecting, that there was gold on their farm. They immediately began blasting in the area of the alleged discovery. In the course of three weeks they sent specimens to an assayer who pronounced the rock capable of producing $10 to $15 a ton. Work was continued during that fall with apparently satisfactory results . . . and it was claimed that specimens assayed as high as $60 a ton. The all-important question now was, "How can the precious metal be extracted?"

It needed money and considerable of it to put the mine into profit . . . . New York parties have recently become interested in the Warren and Fallon mine."

Those New York speculator-operators were Messrs. Rollins and Wilson ("the latter a member of the well-known firm of Wood & Wilson"). They had come to West Windsor to supervise the mining operations after having first obtained "a car-load or two" of the alleged gold-bearing rock, which they then shipped to Newark,

New Jersey. There the ore was roasted, an ore-extracting process to determine the percentage of gold per ton.

So successful had been the salting operation that the sampling was judged "promising." Therefore on January 25, 1887, a warranty bond was given by Benjamin Warren, Carlos L. Fallon, and Mary L. Fallon (wife) to Frank H. Rollins of New York City for the then considerable sum of $20,000 "for the purchase of the rights [only] to enter upon the land . . . and to explore, dig, and carry away any and all minerals therein contained and of working said land and extracting ores therefrom and shipping said ores and operating the mines now or hereafter to be opened thereon."

The unnamed "old miner who chanced to be along that way, and who could not resist to do a little prospecting" was, of course, an accomplice of Warren and Fallon's. He was Stratton Meacham, a gold prospector who had recently returned from California. However, his specialty was salting mines. According to a journal entry of the late historian Mildred Kittridge, Meacham had "filled 2 empty shot gun shells & shot the gold into ledges. . . . Everyone dug for gold but one man became suspicious as all the gold was in one ledge. A sample [was] sent [to] Montpelier & found to be Cal. gold. Meacham admitted his guilt—was sentenced to prison."

Thus West Windsor's mining activities came to an abrupt end. Just as abruptly, Carlos L. Fallon and wife Mary prudently decamped to Fitchburg, Massachusetts; whereas Frank H. Rollins, fleeced but wiser, departed for the less treacherous environment of Manhattan. The municipal court records of the case, stored in the city hall at White River Junction, had been destroyed by fire. So the fate of Warren and Fallon must go unrecorded. Warren stayed on in Sheddsville until his death in 1896. However, a reunion with Fallon occurred on March 23, 1891, when the Fallons returned only long enough to transact the sale of their jointly owned eighty-acre West Windsor farm with its defunct gold mine. Stratton Meacham died in 1904. According to probate records, he left one nephew his gold nugget shirt studs and another his gold nugget scarf pin. Value: two dollars.

Postscript: There still is gold in the area. In 1981, jewelry designer and artisan Paul Gross made his wife's, and his, wedding rings from gold that he panned in a Bridgewater stream.

Chester's Sticky-Fingered Phantom

The safe-cracking at Adams & David Company's Main Street store in Chester one September night in 1886 was the first of over fifty robberies to plague that once placid town for the next sixteen years.

The skill, imagination, and boldness with which the crimes were committed infuriated and frustrated the victims and others, particularly Constable Henry Bond. Nearly all of the stores were burglarized; some at least twice: Burditt Bros., Adams & David Company (three times), Charles Waterman's grist mill (four or five times), and Ware & Sons. Walker's Furniture Company, which had a special sale on those newfangled bicycles that featured uniform-sized wheels, had one disappear through a rear window. Building supplies such as strapped shingles vanished from the local freight depot. Although business enterprises were the prime targets, individuals were not immune. A masked housebreaker prodded farmer George Allen and wife awake with a gun. He then removed $1500 earned from their recent sale of cattle. The phantom thief's favorite victim was James Pollard whose flourishing general store was looted six times. It was such a tempting resource that even the night after Mr. Pollard installed an elaborate burglar alarm, the thief entered via a high 14" x 18" storeroom window and took "a fur coat, a woman's cape and fifteen dollars." The thief eluded successive posses.

The Board of Selectmen, some of whom were victimized merchants, had convened several times, with Constable Bond present, to cuss and discuss the plague of thefts. A $500 reward was offered for information leading to the culprit's arrest. The fever of retribution was so strong that First Selectmen Clarence Adams, owner of a prosperous farm and one of Chester's leading citizens, personally added $100 to the reward. The Board hired a Boston detective who turned out to be an alcoholic. It was reported in the local paper that "the only things he uncovered were several sources of liquor in supposedly dry Chester."

Meanwhile the townspeople were supplied with revolvers that had been specially stocked by druggist F. W. Pierce. But before they were all sold, the phantom burglar broke into the store and exited with the rest.

Logic dictated that several citizens who had police records for petty theft or grand larceny were likely suspects. But the thefts continued after their apprehension, surveillance, or deaths. Because the last entry into Pollard's general store was through such a small window, it was believed that the thief was slight and short. Because Waterman's Mill was so often robbed of feed, it was assumed the robber was either a poor farmer or a ne'er-do-well selling his loot to farmers. These were certainly logical assumptions.

For some townspeople, community action was not enough. Mill-owner Waterman and selectman Clarence Adams surveyed the mill complex together. Afterward they agreed that the thief had removed the mill doors' locks, hasps and all; then, after stealing bags of grain, had reinstalled them. They decided that only by hiring a night watchman would the break-ins be prevented. It worked—until the man was relieved from further duty to save money.

It was the illogical considerations and conjectures that led to a solution. For instance, during the sixteen years of thefts, none of the loot was ever recovered. It was apparent, therefore, that it was not stolen to be sold; that judging by the diversity of the loot, the culprit had little use for much of it. So the burglar was merely a compulsive collector, a "pack rat," possibly a kleptomaniac, therefore a psychopath. His behavior could only be explained in the language of psychiatry. After all, wasn't the basic function of psychiatry to produce logical explanations for aberrant (therefore illogical) behavior?

To bolster this reasoning, Miller Waterman observed that the thief avoided easy or predictable means of entry, preferring ingenious and physically challenging ones that would demonstrate his strength, agility, and resourcefulness while outsmarting and outraging his fellow citizens. Having anticipated the burglar's return visit, Mr. Waterman secretly resorted to a stratagem. Entry, he figured, would be attempted through an almost inaccessible window near the rear of the mill, which was about fifteen feet above the stream. He booby-trapped that window. Access to it could only be gained from the roof of the abutting engine house. He rigged the window with his "mechanical watchman"—a shotgun. Wired to the window sash, its trigger would release only when the lower frame was opened, as it was four nights later on July 29, 1902.

Earlier that evening Mr. Waterman had attended a meeting at the town hall. On his return, he and his family were in the living room, which faced their mill across the road, when they heard a shotgun blast. The miller's young son, Gardner, the only other person who knew of the triggered window, rushed out with his father to fetch Constable Bond. The shotgun had indeed been fired. The window sill was bloodstained. Yet no body was found.

That same night near the base of Clarence Adams's hilltop farmstead, a passerby found Mr. Adams crumpled in the rear of his buckboard, his pants bloodsoaked. He was said to have told his housekeeper, "I've been shot by highwaymen!"

William Dunn, a friend who was visiting that night, fetched the doctor. Mr. Adams's left thigh had been badly mutilated. Eighty-four pieces of #8 buckshot were removed from the wound.

Two crimes in one night, and one of Chester's most popular and prominent citizens the victim of a near-fatal holdup! The townspeople were outraged. Action was demanded. Constable Bond immediately went to work.

It would have been illogical, of course, even preposterous to imagine that a man nearly six feet tall, weighing at least 160 pounds, a genial, bookish, prosperous bachelor farmer whose distinguished record of community service included being an incorporator and trustee of the Chester Savings Bank, a trustee of Chester's Whiting Library, a former chairman of the Board of Selectmen, and who once sat in the Vermont General Assembly as Chester's Town Representative could possibly be Chester's phantom burglar. Yet it did not take Constable Bond long to suspect it. Because at the site near Waterman's Mill where the alleged holdup was said to have occurred, no footprints were recorded in the soft shoulders of the dirt road. Nor was there any blood on the buckboard's seat where Charence Adams claimed he was seated when shot. The blood was in the wagonbed. When the constable showed Mr. Waterman some of the shot that had been dug from Mr. Adams's thigh, the miller said that his mechanical watchman, the shotgun, had indeed been loaded with #8 buckshot.

Of course such evidence was merely circumstantial. So armed with a search warrant and more volunteers than needed, Constable Bond explored Mr. Adams's farm. They found an accumulation of sixteen years' loot. It included grain sacks from Waterman's Mill, bundles of shingles, the new-fangled bicycle from Walker's Furniture Store, the fur coat and woman's cape that had been hauled through the tiny rear window of Pollard's General Store, and the revolvers which druggist Pierce had especially stocked for the townspeople to protect their property from the phantom burglar's rapacious grasp. They even recovered a carton of bow ties, which Adams had stolen from a Montpelier men's shop the year he served in the legislature.

Clarence Adams confessed. Tried at Woodstock, he pleaded guilty. On August 14, 1902, he was given a ten-year sentence to be served at Windsor State Prison.

A closer look at this enigmatic prisoner may reveal what might have predetermined his criminality. Clarence Adams was highly intelligent and personable. His attractiveness was enhanced by meticulous grooming. Although he was financially and socially secure, he was penurious and a loner. Very studious, Mr. Adams was an avid reader of romance and adventure fiction. Yet he never ventured into marriage. About half his library of some two thousand books consisted of crime and detective stories. Could the contrasts of behavior that characterized his own life be attributed, in part, to his well-worn copy of *The Strange Case of Dr. Jekyll and Mr. Hyde*? In early manhood he had sought a career as a Secret Service agent, but his mother "put her foot down." His reading had given him an appetite for travel, a taste he indulged with several trips out west, perhaps to avoid both his responsibilities at the farm and to escape his domineering mother.

Clarence Adams became the prison librarian. He ingratiated himself with Warden Oakes; thus rating small yet significant privileges such as unsupervised visits from William Dunn, his closest friend. Mr. Dunn passed large amounts of Mr. Adams's money to him, the need for which may be evident later. He also befriended a fellow inmate with a medical background who functioned as a jailhouse medic or orderly; and whose association was perhaps cultivated for his advantage—as later events were to suggest. Mr. Adams, who was fascinated by the occult, had acquired the knack of self-hypnosis, a skill which may—or may not—have had some bearing on his alleged death on February 26, 1904. For no less bizarre than his life was his demise.

The circumstances of that death and "burial" sound like a scenario of escape. Consider these facts and their sequence: On February 22, Mr. Adams claimed to be in acute pain from rheumatism (arthritis). It was severe enough for Dr. John Brewster, the visiting physician, to send him to the prison infirmary. There Mr. Adams could be attended to by his prison friend, the orderly.

The second day he had symptoms of the grippe (flu), and predicted his own death. On the twenty-fourth and twenty-fifth Mr. Adams was, or seemed to be worse; so much so that he sent Warden Oakes a formal request that should he die his body was to be prepared by the orderly and then released to Mr. William Dunn.

That Friday, February 26, the orderly notified Dr. Brewster that Mr. Adams had died. According to an account in the *Vermont Journal,* "Apparently without examining the deceased, Dr. Brewster signed the death certificate. Cause of death was given as 'oedema of the lungs' [pneumonia]."

That same afternoon Mr. Adams's body was attended to, in private, solely by his prison orderly friend. On Saturday morning, Mr. Dunn arrived to claim the body. This surprised Warden Oakes because he had not summoned Mr. Dunn who glibly explained that he was merely carrying out the last wishes of his late friend. So the coffin was released to Mr. Dunn who was accompanied by a Windsor undertaker. The body was then taken to a Cavendish cemetery and placed in the above-ground holding vault, to be buried in spring when the ground had sufficiently thawed.

But the saga of Chester's elite burglar was not laid to rest with his alleged burial. For John Greenwood, a reputable Chester acquaintance of Mr. Adams's, said that he had encountered Adams in the Windsor Hotel lobby in Montreal, while on business there, and had a nice chat with him. Later, Mr. Adams was said to have been seen by others in Nova Scotia.

Scarcely a month later, rumors of Mr. Adams's sensational escape had so widely spread that the Hearst papers made a lurid feature story of it. Such a furor resulted that in May the body, presumably Mr. Adams's, was exhumed and examined by a cousin, Frank Adams, and by the cemetery's Sexton Sanders. The relative said that he *thought* it was cousin Clarence. However, the sexton hedged. "I can't say for sure that it was not another body that had been smuggled into the coffin." A cadaver could have been stolen, possibly from Dartmouth College Medical School or from a fresh grave through the efforts of Clarence Adams's good friend, William Dunn, who had disappeared after the alleged entombment. Thus no positive identification was ever made.

The record does not state whether the miller Charles Waterman ever received the $600 reward for his action that had resulted in the brief imprisonment of Clarence Adams, Chester's sticky-fingered phantom, who had donated $100 of that reward for his own apprehension and conviction.

The Snowflake Man

With his lifelong love of snow, Wilson Alwyn Bentley wisely managed to be born in Jericho, where winters in the shadow of Mt. Mansfield have Vermont's heaviest and longest lasting snow-falls.

It was auspicious, then, that on February 9, 1880, his fifteenth birthday, his farmer father and schoolteacher mother gave him an old microscope. Two years later his poor but generous parents presented him with a bellows tripod camera. The microscope had incited an inexhaustible curiosity. As there was snow in abundance, his scrutiny quickly focused on snowflakes. Thus began an obsession of nearly fifty years with his aesthetic and scientific study of snow crystals.

He was not the first to have observed and recorded the patterned structure of snowflakes. Man's awareness of their beauty had been recorded thousands of years earlier. In the Old Testament's Book of Job is the question, "Hast thou entered into the treasures of the snow?" To which contemporary man might justifiably answer, "Yes, through the reverence for the beauty that had inspired 'Snowflake' Bentley's magic eye." In 1555 the Vatican published a book on natural phenomena by Olaus Magnus, the archbishop of Upsala, Sweden, in which he tried, with woodcuts, to illustrate how snowflakes looked. Two hundred and sixty-five years later in

Snowflake montage created by Wilson A. Bentley.

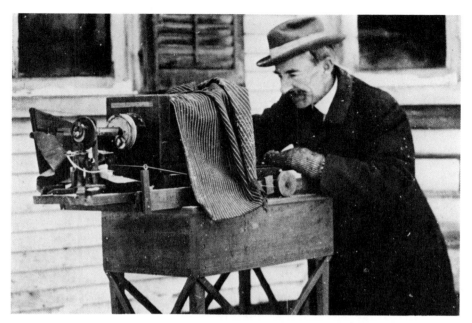

Top: Wilson A. Bentley showing how he used his camera-microscope for snowflake photography. Bottom: Wilson A. Bentley etching out the background of a negative of a snowflake.

1820, William Scoresby, an English arctic explorer, produced drawings of snowflakes.

Yet only with the development of the photographic microscope was it possible to record snowflakes with total clarity and therefore accuracy. This "Snowflake" Bentley accomplished in 1886, when the twenty-one-year old, self-taught scientist produced his first perfect portrait of a snowflake's structure and beauty. He thus had pioneered the technology and art of photomicrography.

A crude shed served as a refrigerated studio for his photomicrographic work. Besides a suitably low temperature, the process required great haste, patience, a steady hand with a delicate touch, and the ability to hold one's breath for at least a minute. The snowflake was "caught" on a soft piece of dust-free black velvet. The camera was poised above it. The contrast of black background with a white snowflake revealed its intricate structure and delicacy. The detail of its outline was made clearer by carefully cutting the image away from the film, and thus freeing it from its background. Even greater detail was achieved by photographing the snowflake on a glass slide with the light projected from beneath by means of a mirror.

From window panes in cold rooms, Bentley's perceptive camera also captured nature's counterfeit of trees, feathers, ferns, lace, coral, and gossamer tracings.

He wrote several treatises on ice crystals and snow. In a 1923 *National Geographic* article, Bentley declared that water was "the life-giving fluid." Whether its form was snow, frost, or dew depended on temperature. "Water molecules," he said, "possess poles, negative and positive, which tend to draw them together in certain alignments forming solids in crystal forms. The number and arrangement of the molecules in crystals determine their pattern. Of all the forms of water," he added, "the tiny six-pointed crystals of ice called 'snow' are the most beautiful and varied." He had discovered the certainty that no two snowflakes are exactly alike, and that all these ice crystals are hexagonal. He further observed that what determined this six-sided shape was that "sixty degree angles are a constant factor in the snowflake's crystalline formation, for that is one sixth of a circle." Bentley was also the first to observe the gradual "blooming" of a snowflake from its tiny nucleus into its ultimate pattern of hexagonal symmetry.

Since "Snowflake" Bentley had revealed the beauty and diversity of these tiny crystals, their potraits have inspired textile and lace manufacturers, wallpaper designers, metal workers, and other craftspeople, especially jewelers. Tiffany Company bought two hundred of his photographs so as to interpret their crystalline patterns with diamonds.

The legacy of the world's greatest authority on snowflakes also enriched the world of science. Although Bentley was mostly self-taught (he never attended high school), he became a Fellow of the American Academy for the Advancement of Science and a member of other learned societies. Originals or reproductions of his 5800 known microphotos are owned by natural history museums, colleges, and universities throughout the world. Harvard's Peabody Museum has its Bentley plates on permanent exhibition. Many of his illustrated articles appeared in national and foreign magazines. In 1931 his book, *Snow Crystals,* (co-authored by W. J. Humphrey of the U. S. Weather Bureau), which pictures 2453 snowflakes, became the definitive work on the subject of snow and ice crystals.

However much happiness and fame his snowflakes gave him, the profit was negligible. To augment his meager income from farming, he gave "magic lantern slide" lectures on his work, sold photographs and slides, and wrote articles.

Until his death at sixty-six on Christmas Eve, 1931, "Snowflake" Bentley, a bachelor, lived in the same farmhouse in which he was born. He did his own housekeeping in the monastic seclusion of three rooms he had reserved for himself and his studies, but shared the farm work with his married brother whose family lived in the rest of the house. However, this modest little man—he was less than five feet tall—was no recluse. He enjoyed the warmth of sociability and was popular. His first and only love, however, was for his Vermont snowflakes which he made internationally famous.

Vermont's Invention Pioneers: The VIP's of Genius

Protruding from the lawn of Springfield's Hartness mansion (now an inn) is not an interplanetary rocket poised for a twenty-first century space rendezvous. It is inventor James Hartness's observatory. It is reached by a subterranean serpentine tunnel off which, like tendrils on a vine, are a workshop-laboratory, a study, a sitting room with bathroom, and finally the observatory. But astronomy was just a hobby; the universe was only one of James Hartness's spheres of interest. Technology was his world, and the rewards of his labors in that labyrinth of scientific research and experimentation were over 100 patents. His prodigious output of inventions has been recorded in a five-page catalog.

Vermont is said to have produced more inventors per capita than any other state. The reason is apparent in the fact that invention is the byproduct of necessity. Survival demanded self-reliance. Vermont's rugged terrain, few natural resources, and harsh climate bred in its stubborn sons an inventive genius that produced an awesome crop of inventions. They have influenced and enriched all mankind.

The scope of inventions by Vermonters reflects the growth of the country, even before Vermont became one of its member states. In 1790 the United States' first patent was issued to Burlington's Samuel Hopkins for a potash-making process. Potash, derived from lye, is made from the leaching of ashes of select hardwoods from which soap and glass were produced. It was Vermont's first cash crop. Hopkins' patent was signed by George Washington and Thomas Jefferson. Shortly afterward, Congress passed an act that excluded foreigners from receiving patents. This included Vermonters, who were not United States citizens until a year later when Vermont joined the nation as its fourteenth state.

The Vermont settlers' first mechanical appliance was the pumping mill, a corncrusher invented by Arlington's Remember Baker. Its success led to one of America's early industries, the community grist mill, which mushroomed along or over New England streams and harnessed the water power. Baker was also the first Vermonter to build a grist and sawmill. Such mills were so important to the town's economy that the state offered a subsidy to whomever built and operated one.

Enterprising Matthew Lyon, who was in his teens when he arrived from Ireland as an indentured servant, also exemplifies the settlers' genius and self-reliance. When he became a printer in 1785, he produced his own paper by inventing a process of making it from the plentiful supply of basswood bark. Lyon also built an iron foundry whose smelters and forges were fueled by bog iron, dug in the town of Sheldon.

An early incentive for inventing is attributed to the colonists' resistance to England's demand that her colonies purchase manufactured goods only from England. This restriction inflamed the colonists' dissatisfaction with England and, along with other repressive measures, helped to ignite the Revolution. However, the era of mechanical inventions in which Vermonters were such notable achievers was precipitated by the War of 1812 and its trade embargo. Before that, England was the principal source of quality tools and machinery.

Yet a later impetus of Vermonters' unique creativity came from alien soil, "alien" because it existed south of the border, and was foreign to Vermont's farm-oriented economy. That compulsive force was America's industrial revolution. The growing demand for industrial products and consumer goods was a challenge that promised seemingly unlimited frontiers of opportunity, especially after the accelerated reach of the railroads made the country an accessible market for Vermont's manufactured goods. Indeed, if necessity was the mother of invention, opportunity was the father.

"The cradle of American industry" is said to have been Springfield. The diversity of its inventions range from the industrial and commercial to agricultural machinery and appliances to consumer goods. For instance, sheep-raising became a profitable enterprise after the importation of 3,900 Merino sheep from Portugal into Vermont, in 1810, by Weathersfield's William Jarvis who was the United States consul in Lisbon. As a result, the manufacturing of textile machinery became one of Springfield's specialties. Partners John Davidson and Frank Parks met the challenge for efficiency by patenting a machine for "finishing" woolen cloth. They also produced a vibrating sheep-shearing machine; and they eased the chores of women by inventing a rotary churn.

A short roster selected from the over two hundred patents that were issued to Springfield inventors should amply justify that city's distinction as having been the capital of American invention: Frank Dresser's braces for cripples; Joel Ellis's steam shovel (1848) and jointed dolls; Edwin Fellows, the founder of the historic Fellows Corporation, produced the gear-cutting machine (1898); Isaac Fisher, Jr.'s milled cotton cloth and sandpaper; A. G. Fullam's hair clippers; and A. W. Gray's endless chain horse-power machine. James Hartness's flat turret lathe (1892) revolutionized the machine tool industry. S. Hill was heralded by the dairy industry for his milk cooler, as was Abner Totles for an evaporator. Noah Safford's hay cutter was a boon to farmers, as was Jesse Warren's land plow that bears his name.

As for other Springfield VIP's of genius: Horace Smith invented "the only lock that cannot be picked" (as his ads proclaimed). He also invented the wooden split clothespin, the hook-and-eye fastener, a corn planter, and an adding machine. He is best remembered as the Smith of Smith and Wesson's famous breech-loading rifle.

If Springfield was the cradle of American industry, Windsor and little West Windsor could claim to have shared in rocking it with the momentum of their sons' inventive genius. Consider these bench marks of technological progress: Windsor's Lemuel

Hodge patented a band saw and the folding rule. In 1815 he invented a method to rule blank paper, and received a patent for a revolving machine that made the process possible. In 1827 Thomas Pomeroy patented an "engine for dividing scales," thus creating a method to standardize the manufacture of quality production. Lysander Rice devised a roller process for grinding flour, and John M. Cooper improvised the Cooper rotative piston pump. In 1828, West Windsor's Ashabel Hubbard patented a revolving hydraulic pump. He was related to Windsor's George W. Hubbard, who had married Ashabel's daughter and produced a dynasty of inventors. George Hubbard patented the nation's first coffee percolator. Perhaps these Hubbards were kin of brothers Elias and Asa Hubbard who perfected a suspension scale and a counter scale with detachable scoop.

Vermont-bred gunsmiths were designers and manufacturers of famous American firearms. The need for weapons was threefold. The first was for game. While the settlers were cultivating the land to raise crops and livestock, game was vital to their subsistence living. The second was for use in "the winning of the West." The third was for firepower to wage the War of 1812, the Mexican-American War (1846-1848), the Civil War, and the Spanish-American War of 1898.

Windsor became a thriving gun manufacturing center. The Kendall Rifle was invented by West Windsor's Nicanor Kendall. Chester's Richard Smith Lawrence, together with Benjamin Henry, improved the Jennings Repeating Rifle. Known as the "Henry Rifle," it was famous for its use in the Civil War. It became the Winchester Rifle when Governor Winchester founded the manufacturing company bearing his name.

In partnership with Horace Smith, Daniel Wesson got a patent for a breech-loading rifle. Wesson was its inventor and Smith financed its production. The partnership was incorporated as the famous Smith and Wesson Company. Today, sequestered in the remote hills of Tunbridge is Daniel Wesson's great-great grandson. Daniel Wesson III is a designer-manufacturer who does custom machine-tooling. His inventions are not limited to gunsmithing. His engineering expertise, which has literally spilled over into molded plastics, has produced a reel for sportsmen known as

DATS, which stands for Decoy Anchor-Tender System.

Old Daniel Wesson had a competitor. Christian Sharpe patented another breech-loading rifle, which was manufactured in Windsor in 1848. Other Vermont gunsmiths were Hiram Berdan who invented the Berdan Rifle; Albert Bell, the Bell Repeating Rifle; and William Palmer, the Palmer Carbine. Fourteen years before Connecticut's Samuel Colt made his six-shooter, that identical weapon was manufactured in Brattleboro.

There are other spurious claims to invention "firsts." Historians concede that the steamboat Robert Fulton built in 1807 was neither the first nor was Fulton its inventor. For in 1793—fourteen years earlier—Samuel Morey of Fairlee successfully operated his steamboat on the Connecticut River. It was a ferry that shuttled between Fairlee, Vermont, and Orford, New Hampshire. A year later he operated one from Hartford, Connecticut, to Manhattan Island. Discouraged by business reverses, he was said to have sunk his original steamboat in the lake at Fairlee that bears his name.

Thomas Davenport, a Brandon blacksmith, devised an electric telegraph apparatus. But in 1834 Professor Samuel F. B. Morse simplified it and constructed an alphabet for its use—the Morse Code. Morse achieved wealth and fame for his alleged invention. Meanwhile, back in his shop, Davenport invented an electric piano and an electric railroad. His most notable achievement was the invention of an electromagnetic motor. It was a rotating machine with revolving and fixed electromagnets, and is the basis of the dynamos that generate power to produce energy and motion.

Professor Alonzo Jackman of Norwich University devised the first ocean cable in 1842. Ignorant of or indifferent to the turbulence of business promotion and exploitation, he generously published how it was made, and the process by which one could link continents with it—a reality that was achieved eleven years later by Cyrus W. Field who reaped fame and wealth for its conception and creation.

Whether Swedish-born John Ericsson or Bennington's John T. Wilson was the designer of the Monitor, America's first iron-clad ship of Civil War fame, is disputed. And, in 1876 Chelsea's Phineas Bailey published a phonetic system of shorthand writing. Yet eighteen years later Isaac Pitman was credited with having invented a system which is almost identical to Bailey's.

St. Johnsbury's Thaddeus Fairbanks patented a revolutionary iron plow in 1826. Its basic concept and design are still in use. However, he is best known for his platform scale. Originally it was designed to weigh hemp, which was then a profitable cash crop. In addition to store and warehouse use, it was adapted for weighing wagonloads, canal boats, and trains. It was on a Fairbanks scale that the portly Aga Khan was weighed annually, and the pounds were calibrated into their value in diamonds or gold. That sum was then distributed to the poor. In 1840, Mr. Fairbanks bought from brothers Elias and Asa Hubbard their patents for a suspension scale plus a counter scale with detachable scoop, in order to expand the Fairbanks Company's product lines.

Frank A. Strong of Vergennes also patented a scale. It was the ball bearing platform scale which was manufactured by John Howe, first in Brandon, then in Rutland. The John Howe Scale Company made aircraft-weighing scales. They even weighed World War II's B-24's, a hefty 250 tons each.

Another blacksmith-turned-inventor besides Brandon's Thomas Davenport was John Deere of Rutland. He had dropped out of Middlebury College to test his mettle as a mechanic. In 1837 he forged his mechanical aptitude and business acumen to invent and produce the world's first steel moldboard plow, known as "the plow that broke the plains." He left Vermont for the West where he founded the empire known as the John Deere Farm Machinery Company.

Vermont's granite and marble industry has long been one of the state's major economic resources. It once flourished in Danby, Dorset, Rutland, Sutherland Falls, Middlebury, and West Windsor. The largest, most productive quarries are still in Proctor and Barre. As early as 1803, Middlebury's marble quarry was the first to use Hiram Kimball's marble saw, and Otto Ulrickson's marble planer.

Finally, the name Henry M. Leland commands respect and induces nostalgia among antique auto buffs. Besides having invented a bevel gear-grinder (1896), he was the designer-engineer of the Lincoln automobile which was then known as the Leland-Lincoln.

It is axiomatic that, in addition to the profit motive, the incentive for invention was to better the quality of life by making productivity more efficient, by making products faster in greater quantity and better quality, and at less cost and labor. Ultimately Vermont inventors enhanced the amenities of life for a greater number of people. Such was the miracle of the industrial revolution. For despite the often shameful exploitation of workers, its benefits were everywhere evident. Consider this sampling of additional inventions: William B. Clapp was the innovator of commercial meat canning, and William W. Chandler invented the refrigerator car. The Reverend John A. Dodge's domestic sewing machine was a blessing to women, and Charles I. Baker's apple parer was no less welcome. For leisure, Joseph T. Buel produced his still popular spoon fishing lure, and Brattleboro's Joseph Estey invented and manufactured the famous Estey Organ. Besides J. Henry Frenier's mowing machine and several industrial inventions, he devised a velocipede (bicycle). His bicycle provided transportation that, because of its solid rubber tires, was practically maintenance-free; it also delighted generations of children and adults as a free-wheeling recreational vehicle. The Otis Elevator was perfected by Halifax's Elisha Graves Otis. For the numerous do-it-yourself craftsmen and millwrights, Middlebury's Jeremiah Hall's circular saw, Shaftsbury's Silas Howes' steel carpenter's square and flexible shaft, and the first wood-planing machine, invented by Alburg's Joseph S. Mott, were a welcome benefit.

American ingenuity, from which so much of the world's sophisticated technology has sprung, is exemplified by the preeminence of Vermont's invention-pioneers. Their self-reliance, resourcefulness and skill have indeed influenced and enriched mankind by freeing men's—and women's—hands, backs, and feet to achieve that not-impossible dream of progress through technology.

The Vermont Mystique

A Philosophical Speculation
on the Making of a Vermonter

No autopsy could reveal what differentiates a typical Vermonter from forty-nine other breeds of U. S. citizens. One reason is that, far from being defunct, Vermonters are a hardy body of Americans whose uniqueness resists analysis. Another reason is that a real Vermonter would scoff at the "typical" label. Close folk, they are too independent to be uniformly stereotyped.

Yet no less real for being elusive, Vermonters do invite and deserve the scrutiny of historians, social scientists, and those who, as recent immigrants, delve into their lore and psyche with the zeal of converts. The following comments are the observations and speculations of such a convert.

Dorothy Canfield Fisher, a Vermonter by adoption (but whose family tree has Vermont roots), listed as the principal ingredients of the Vermont character "individual freedom, personal independence, human dignity, community responsibility, social and political democracy, sincerity, restraint in outward conduct, and thrift." Specific manifestations of these general attributes will serve to illustrate and illuminate aspects of Vermont's psyche and history. (For what is history but the recorded dynamics of behavior that shaped the destiny of man?)

It was "personal independence" and "human dignity" that moved destitute and infirm old Seth Chase to declare "I'll starve or freeze to death there [in the woods] before I'll go to that accursed poorhouse!" His predicament revealed the inadequacy of Vermont's early welfare facilities and procedures.

It was also the imperative for "personal independence" and "human dignity" that incited a conspiracy of freedom-loving lawyers, judges, doctors, bankers, clergymen, businessmen, and other prominent (and mostly anonymous) citizens to forge an escape route the width and length of Vermont for slaves fleeing to Canada. Not all the fugitives completed their trek. Among those who chose to stay in their host state were some who fought in the Union Army.

"Personal independence" was paramount in the unique life and accomplishments of loner "Snowflake" Bentley. The beauty and scientific truths revealed in the life-long studies of Jericho's self-taught naturalist were a triumph of independent spirit. Indeed, his work confirmed Keats's assertion that "beauty is truth, truth beauty."

It is no coincidence that the ingredients of Vermont character, listed by Mrs. Fisher, so well define the essence of eccentricity. For "individual freedom" is to eccentrics what sap is to sugar maples. That is not to dismiss Vermont's bumper crop of eccentrics as sappy. Many were admired; a few were envied; some were ludicrous; while all, as eccentrics, were the embodiment of integrity.

Vermonters were, and are, compulsive free-thinkers. This accounts for the fact that the state produced four home-grown religions. Their founders were: Joseph Dorril, leader of the Dorrilites; William Miller, whose followers were known as the Millerites; Sharon's Joseph Smith, founder of the Church of Jesus Christ of Latter-day Saints (whose followers are the Mormons); and Putney's John Humphrey Noyes whose converts to his "perfectionism" were known as members of the Oneida Community.

Of the many instances of Vermonters' "human dignity," none is more poignant than how young Private William Scott exemplified Hemingway's definition of courage as "grace under pressure" when the Groton lad faced death. Or how Ann Story, facing the danger of the wilderness, survived not only a hostile environment, but the depredations of several Indian raids.

As for "community responsibility (and) social and political

democracy," proof of these characteristics could not be more evident in one time and place than at an annual Town Meeting, which is held in some 242 communities. The impact of Vermont character manifested in this exercise of democracy is an awesome thing. Consider the following incident: A proposal to re-assess all property at 100 percent of value was amended to have the basis of evaluation realistically determined by land use. Such zoning would, of course, benefit the farmer. Otherwise the profit from his productivity, directly related to the amount of his arable or grazing acreage, would be disproportionately taxed. Yet the farmers voted against such advantageous zoning. Why? Because nobody was going to dictate what they could or could not do with their land. Property is inviolate; ownership sacred. Zoning, they felt, was a threat to their "individual freedom, their personal independence." The decision of these "old-timers" reflected the dominance of principle over expediency. Ironically, the new-comers, no less eager to preserve the rural ambiance of the Ver-mont way of life, were strong advocates of restrictive (and in this instance, preferential) zoning.

However, just as there may have been Vermonters who were slave-owning Judge Stephen Jacob's peers in perversity, the exer-cise of folly as an act of "community responsibility," was once so prevalent that, like measles, it had infected a whole town, as it did Glover where an effort to bring water to its mills nearly de-stroyed the town.

Admittedly the Vermont character is not a specific, but rather is a composite, just as Vermont's communities once were defined by the topographical diversity of the four corners that locked them into four watersheds. Socio-physical divergencies were therefore inevitable. Yet this very localism spawned the strong individuality and assertive independence of its citizens. So certain aspects of the state's geography and climate significantly influenced their character.

Of New England's six states only Vermont is devoid of seacoast. It remains the most rural. Until the late 1930's, poor roads made the Green Mountains an effective barrier dividing the state's east and west portions. It was justifiably called "the back country."

Nearly two-thirds of it is forest-covered. This limitation plus the problem of rocky, thin topsoil, a short growing season (varying from 150 days in the Champlain valley to the Connecticut valley's 120 days), and long, cold winters with an average snowfall of 7.5 feet make an obviously inhospitable terrain and climate. It was a challenge that imposed disciplines which bred hardiness, industry, resourcefulness, independence, and thrift.

In short, the ethic of work was the gospel of survival.

It was no coincidence that in such an environment the deep roots of the Protestant ethic held the Vermonter to his harsh land with the certainty that the fruits of his sacrifice and labor would be the Almighty's reward of material success. This promise was not only thundered from the pulpit. Its premise was dogmatically echoed in the classroom. This was not surprising, because ministers frequently augmented their meager salaries by teaching. Elder Ariel Kendrick, Baptist minister from Woodstock, justified such "moonlighting" by asserting "those who preach by the gospel should labor by it." Another teacher-minister was Fairfield's William Arthur, father of our twenty-first president. They brought the tenets of Calvinistic morality into the classroom with evangelical fervor.

The best example of Calvinism's long and pervasive influence is the phenomenon of *The McGuffey Reader.* From 1836 to 1857 over 120,000,000 copies of the clergyman-educator William Holmes McGuffey's *Eclectic Reader* indoctrinated pupils of the first six grades in the prevailing moral, social, cultural, and political norms. The pedagogic material of the illustrated series and its sermonizing style set a precedent that was popular well into the 1880's. The public schools were strong purveyors of the Protestant ethic. Social conduct and moral precepts were encapsuled in dialogues, which were akin to parables, and frequently Bible-oriented. For instance, "The meek shall inherit the earth" was interpreted to teach the virtue and rewards of goodness.

Morality, as taught by the seemingly militant dictates of Protestantism, was the concern, if not the responsibility, of public education. McGuffey's success as a writer in this medium and his many imitators made the material as durable as it was unique. The process of rote and catechistic teaching dominated grammar school classrooms for decades. Horace Mann, a contemporary of McGuffey's, advocated the use of the Bible in public schools as a suitable text for morality and citizenship. In the context of the Protestant ethic, citizenship was the exercise of social conscience and humanitarianism that translated the rewards of Christian living into democracy's blessings. In short, free enterprise (that is, capitalism) was not only sanctioned, it was a testament of faith.

The Protestant ethic's influence on Vermont education was spread nationwide through the gospel of a Burlington-born philosopher and educator, John Dewey, known as the prophet of progressive education. His cult of *experimentation* and *pragmatism* expressed the Vermont character. For an individual's freedom was obligatory in the pursuit of truth, and enlightenment could only be achieved in an environment of personal independence in the framework of political and social democracy.

Inevitably, the pendulum of reaction swung vigorously. Calvinism, in the sombre, tight frockcoat of Congregationalism, receded in the passing procession of Protestantism. Ethan Allen voiced the reaction against the political and socio-economic dominance of the "Standing Order Clergy" (Congregational) in his ponderous diatribe, *Oracles of Reason.*

The anti-Calvinist movement was in historian I. Woodbridge Riley's phrase "a recoil from Puritanism." However, its movement was primarily secular, not religious. Yet such dissent, particularly stemming from political philosophy, was frowned upon as subversive. Thus between 1791 and 1850 proponents of a "natural rights liberalism"—today it would be labeled "civil rights" liberalism—opposed the Calvinist system of election and reprobation. "Election" here meant not by the ballot box but by the privilege of birth, position, and religious credentials. "Natural rights liberalism" was manifested in a vigorously independent spirit and character, a political assertiveness and autonomy that shaped Vermont's history and character. The inhabitants of the New Hampshire Grants, then the geographic reference to Vermont, resisted the blandishments of New York, Maine, and Massachusetts, rejected any sovereignty but their own, and became the independent State of Vermont. That was in 1777. For fourteen years it remained free, joining the new nation in 1791 as the fourteenth state.

Freedom and Unity is emblazoned on the state's emblem. Although the motto was chosen in 1862, Vermonters have tradi-
tionally and amply exemplified both concepts. Not only did Vermont early assert its independence and protect its freedom against
the incursions of neighbors, but of all the states' constitutions,
only Vermont's prohibited slavery. The most liberal of its era, it
also "granted all adult male citizens the right to vote without regard to race, religion, or the ownership of property." One ingredient of freedom is integrity. To become a voter, a Vermonter
still must take an oath—rightly named the Freeman's Oath— to
vote "without fear or favor of any person."

Striking proof of the Vermonters' choice to act on principle
rather than expediency was their participation in the Civil War.
Consider these statistics as proof of their commitment to *Freedom
and Unity:* Per capita, more Vermonters fought than any other
Northerners; 34,555 to be exact. This was one in every four of
the entire male population. Of these, only 2,954, or less than 10
percent, were drafted. Vermont's total cash contribution during
the Civil War was $9,323,407.50—no mere pittance for a people
whose frugality was legendary.

About 1824, over-optimistic prospects for cash crops resulted
in a shift to sheep-raising, and later to dairy farming. The Vermonters met the challenge and promise of the Industrial Revolution. The mushrooming of small mills in the nineteenth century
and the rampant growth of the machine-tool industry into the
twentieth century, were the result of Yankee enterprise, ingenuity,
and inventiveness. Per capita, there were more inventions patented
by Vermonters during this era than in any other state.

The terrible loss of manpower caused by the Civil War accelerated the immigration, begun in the early 1850's, of laborers to
build the railroads, man the farms, textile, lumber, and wood-
working mills, the quarries and factories. These immigrants,
mostly French-Canadians and southern Europeans, were Catholic.
Their presence created a religious and ethnic heterogeneity. Although "foreign," it enriched—rather than diluted—the Vermont
character.

Speaking of his beloved birthplace, the usually restrained Calvin
Coolidge said in a 1928 speech at Bennington, "If the spirit of

liberty should vanish in other parts of the Union and support of our institutions should languish, it could all be replenished from the generous store held by the people of this brave little state of Vermont."

A relevant postscript might be a reference to the obvious influence of Coolidge's background as a native Vermonter. He had won national prominence when, as governor of Massachusetts, he translated the precepts of Calvinistic morality into terms of law and order to end the Boston police strike with his famous dictum, "There is no right to strike against the public safety by anybody, anywhere, anytime." After President Harding's verbose pomposity, political flamboyance, and immorality, and the rampant corruption in his administration, the nation welcomed Calvin Coolidge's no-nonsense simplicity and rectitude. His popularity was a tacit acknowledgment that the Protestant ethic, evident in his character and career, illuminated the Vermont mystique.